The Pocket Guide to
Critical Thinking

Richard L. Epstein

Wadsworth
Thomson Learning™

Australia • Canada • Mexico • Singapore
Spain • United Kingdom • United States

Philosophy Editor: *Peter Adams*
Editorial Assistant: *Mindy Newfarmer*
Assistant Editor: *Kerri Abdinoor*
Marketing Manager: *David Garrison*
Development Editor: *Alan Venable*
Cover Design: *Carole Lawson*
Cartoons: *Alex Raffi*

Research for this project was supported by the
Advanced Reasoning Forum.

Printed in the United States of America
1 2 3 4 5 6 7 03 02 01 00 99

For permission to use material from this text, contact us by
Web: http://www.thomsonrights.com
Fax: 1-800-730-2215
Phone: 1-800-730-2214

For more information, contact:
Wadsworth/Thomson Learning
10 Davis Drive
Belmont, CA 94002–3098
USA
www.wadsworth.com

ISBN 0-534-55844-5

Preface

This little book is meant as a summary and guide to the art of reasoning well in daily life.

Critical thinking is evaluating whether we should be convinced that some claim is true or some argument is good, as well as formulating good arguments. Critical thinking is something we need to do every day.

I've summarized here the most important ideas about the subject. But critical thinking is more than knowing definitions and rules and a few examples. It requires judgment. The full story, with motivation and lots of examples and exercises is in my textbook *Critical Thinking*. Use this *Pocket Guide* as a place to start learning how to reason well and write good arguments or as a summary for reference. Your practice can come from using these ideas every day watching television, reading the newspaper, talking to your friends, working at your job, raising your children.

The short chapters here can be read more or less independently, though a familiarity with the material up through Chapter 6 on repairing arguments is assumed in all the following chapters.

Because your reasoning can be sharpened, you can understand more, you can avoid being duped. You can reason well with those you love and work with and need to convince. And, we hope, you will make better decisions. But whether you will do so depends not just on method, not just on the tools of reasoning, but on your goals, your ends. And that depends on virtue.

1 Claims

Reasoning well begins with being able to recognize and make claims and definitions.

> **Claim** A declarative sentence that we can view as either true or false (but not both).

Dogs are mammals. *Claim.*

$2 + 2 = 5$ *Claim.*

Dick is hungry. *Claim.*

How can anyone be so dumb as to think that cats can reason?
Not a claim. Questions aren't claims.

I wish I were taller.
Not a claim. Prayers and wishes are not claims, though someone could claim he is wishing.

Todo cachorro pode latir.
Claim? If you don't understand it, don't reason with it.

> **Vague Sentences** A sentence which has no clear way to understand it.

If we can't understand what someone is saying, how can we say that it is true or false? But in order to communicate, almost every sentence we use is going to be somewhat vague. The issue is not whether a sentence is vague, but whether it is *too vague* to be a claim.

1

Too vague
You can win a lot playing blackjack.
Our dish soap is new and improved.
People who are disabled are just as good as people who aren't.

Drawing the line   It's a mistake to argue that if you can't make the difference precise, there is no difference.

If a suspect who is totally uncooperative is hit once by a policeman, then that's not unnecessary force. Nor twice, if he's resisting. Possibly three times. If he's still resisting, shouldn't the policeman have the right to hit him again? It would be dangerous not to allow that. So, you can't tell me exactly how many times a policeman has to hit a suspect before it's unnecessary force. So the defendant did not use unnecessary force. *This is drawing the line: just because you can't say precisely what unnecessary force is doesn't mean you can't recognize it in the extremes.*

Objective Claim   A claim that is true independently of what anyone or any thing thinks / believes / feels. It invokes **impersonal standards**.

Subjective Claim   A claim that is not objective. It invokes **personal standards**.

Suppose Harry says:

"New cars today are really expensive."

If Harry means that new cars cost too much for him to feel comfortable buying one, then the claim is subjective. If Harry has in mind that the average cost of a new car is more than twice the federal government poverty standard for a family of four, then he would be using impersonal standards, and it is objective. Or Harry may have no standard in mind, in which case it's too vague to be a claim.

If it is not clear what standard is being invoked, don't argue about the claim. The sentence is too vague.

All ravens are black.   *Objective*

My dog is hungry.   *Subjective.*

It's cold outside.
Subjective claim. Too vague to be an objective claim.

Wanda weighs 215 lbs. *Objective.*

Wanda is fat. *Subjective.*

Abortion is wrong.
Not a claim. Too vague, unless meant as subjective. Wrong according to what standard?

I'm feeling romantic tonight.
Too vague. This isn't even clear enough to be a subjective claim.

Confusing objective and subjective It's a mistake to treat a subjective claim as objective, or vice versa.

— That tie is hideous. I'm not going to a party with you like that.
— What are you talking about? This tie is great. It's the style.
— You're crazy. It's ugly.

— (Student) I deserve a higher mark in this course.
— (Teacher) No you don't.
— (Student) That's just your opinion.

> **Ambiguous Sentence** A sentence which has at least two clear ways to understand it.
>   An ambiguous sentence is never a claim.

Ambiguous
Zoe saw the waiter with the glasses.
Dr. E's dogs eat over 10 pounds of meat every week.
   (Ambiguous between the group and the individual: Each dog or all the dogs together eat that much?)

   An ambiguous sentence can't be a claim before we decide which way to understand it.

> **Definition** An explanation or stipulation of how to use a word or phrase.

   Definitions are not claims. They are not true or false, but good or bad, apt or wrong. A **persuasive definition** is a claim masquerading as a definition. For example: "Abortion is the murder of unborn children." What should be debated is being assumed in the definition. Beware of and do not use persuasive definitions.

"Dog" means "domestic canine". *Definition.*

Puce is the color of a flea, purple brown or brownish purple. *Definition.*

A dog is a man's best friend.
Not a definition. Not a claim, either, because it's too vague.

A feminist is someone who thinks that women are better than men. *Persuasive definition.*

— Maria's so rich, she can afford to buy you dinner.
— What do you mean by "rich"?
— She's got a Mercedes.
Not a definition (or a very bad one). Some people who have Mercedes aren't rich, and some people who are rich don't own one. That Maria has a Mercedes is some *evidence* that she's rich.

The type A person is one who exhibits the following behavioral characteristics: constant hurriedness, free-floating hostility, and intense competitiveness.
Bad definition. The words doing the defining are too vague.

In a ***good definition*** the words doing the defining are clear and better understood than the word or phrase being defined; and it's correct to use the defining words exactly when it's correct to use the word or phrase being defined.

Steps in making a good definition
1. Show the need for a definition.
2. State the definition.
3. Make sure the words make sense.
4. Give examples where the definition applies.
5. Give examples where the definition does not apply.
6. If necessary, contrast it with other likely definitions.
7. Possibly revise your definition.

2　Concealed Claims

> Someone tries to convince us by his choice of words rather than an argument—the subtleties of rhetoric in place of reasoned deliberation.

> **Slanter**　Any literary device that attempts to convince by using words that conceal a dubious claim.

Slanters are bad because they try to get us to assume a dubious claim is true without reflecting on it. Below are various kinds of slanters.

> **Loaded Question**　A question that conceals a dubious claim that should be argued for rather than assumed.

When are you planning to start working hard?
Why don't you love me anymore?
Why can't you dress like a gentleman?

The best response to a loaded question is to point out the concealed claim and begin discussing that.

> **Euphemism**　(yoo'-fuh-mizm) A word or phrase that makes something sound better than a neutral description.
>
> **Dysphemism**　(dis'-fuh-mizm) A word or phrase that makes something sound worse than a neutral description.

"Freedom fighter"—the guerillas are good people fighting to liberate their country and give their countrymen freedom.

"Terrorist"—the guerillas are bad people, inflicting violence on civilians for their own partisan ends without popular support.

> ***Downplayer***   A word or phrase that minimizes the significance of a claim.
>
> ***Up-player***   A word or phrase that exaggerates the significance of a claim.

Zoe: Hey Mom. Great news. I managed to pass my first French exam.

Mom: You only just passed?

Zoe has up-played the significance of what she did, concealing the claim "It took great effort to pass" with the word "managed." Her mother downplayed the significance of passing by using "only just," concealing the claim "Passing and not getting an A is not commendable."

One way to downplay is with words that restrict or limit the meaning of others, what we call *qualifiers*—like the asterisks in advertisements. For instance, I can sell you a house in Cedar City for only $18,000.*

A *weaseler* is a claim that's qualified so much that the apparent meaning is no longer there.

Dick (to his boss): I am truly sorry that it has taken so long for you to understand what I have been saying.

> ***Proof Substitute***   A word or phrase that suggests the speaker has a proof, but no proof is actually offered.

Dr. E: By now you must have been convinced what a great teacher I am. It's obvious to anyone. Of course, some people are a little slow. But surely you see it.

---

*On approved credit and $500 down and the right to your first-born child.

Dr. E didn't prove that he is a great teacher, though he made it sound as if he were proving something. He was just reiterating the claim, trying to browbeat you into believing it with the words "obvious," "some people are slow," "surely," "must have been convinced."

Another way to conceal that you have no support for your claim is to *shift the burden of proof.*

— You should vote for Senator Ruiz.
— Why?
— Why not?

Any concealed claim is an *innuendo*. But usually we use that term for concealed claims that are really unpleasant.

— Where are you from?
— New York.
— Oh, I'm sorry.

You may be tempted to use slanters in your own writing. Don't. Slanters turn off those you want to convince—it's like preaching to the converted. Worse, though they may work for the moment, they don't stick. Without reinforcement, the other person will remember only the joke or jibe. A good argument can last and last—the other person can see the point clearly and reconstruct it. And if you use slanters, your opponent can destroy your points not by facing your real argument, but by pointing out the slanters.

> If you reason calmly and rationally you will earn the respect of the other, and may learn that the other merits your respect, too.

3 Arguments

> An *argument* is a collection of claims, one of
> which is called the *conclusion*, whose truth
> the argument is intended to establish. The
> others are called the *premises*, which are
> supposed to lead to, or support, or convince
> that the conclusion is true.

The point of an argument is to convince that a claim—
the conclusion—is true. The conclusion is sometimes
called the *issue* that is being debated.

You should study critical thinking because you will be able to
reason better and it will help you get a job.
Premises: If you study critical thinking you will be able to reason
better. Studying critical thinking will help you get a job.
Conclusion: You should study critical thinking.

Sheep are the dumbest animals. If the one in front walks off a cliff,
all the rest will follow. And if they get rolled on their backs, they
can't right themselves.
Premises: If the sheep in front walks off a cliff, all the rest will
follow. If sheep get rolled on their backs, they can't right
themselves. *Conclusion*: Sheep are the dumbest animals.

Out? Out? I was safe by a mile. Are you blind? He didn't even
touch me with his glove!
Premise: He didn't even touch me with his glove.
Conclusion: I was safe.
(The rest is noise.)

Follow the directions for using this medicine provided by your doctor. This medicine may be taken on an empty stomach or with food. Store this medicine at room temperature, away from heat and light.
Not an argument. Instructions or commands are not an attempt to convince anyone that some claim is true.

How come you don't call me? What's wrong? You don't love your mother? Where did I go wrong?
Not an argument. Not every attempt to persuade is an attempt to convince that a claim is true.

> ***Indicator Word***   A word or phrase added to a claim to tell us the role of the claim in an argument or what the speaker thinks of the claim or argument.

Conclusion indicators: hence; therefore; so; thus; consequently; we can then show that; it follows that; . . .

Premise indicators: since; because; for; in as much as; given that; suppose that; it follows from; on account of; due to; . . .

Indicators of speaker's belief: probably; certainly; most likely; I think; . . .

A claim is ***dubious*** or ***implausible*** if we have no good reason to believe that it is true, yet are not sure it's false. If we know that a claim is true or have very good reason to believe it is true, we'll say the claim is ***highly plausible***.

> ***Good Argument***   An argument where the premises give good reason to believe the conclusion is true.

What do we mean by "good reason"? For an argument to be good, it must pass two tests:
• There should be good reason to believe the premises.
• The premises lead to, support, establish the conclusion.

In Chapter 4 we'll look at criteria for what counts as good reason to accept a premise. In Chapter 5 we'll spell out what we mean for a conclusion to follow from the premises. But here we can already note that these two tests are independent of each other:

Premises and conclusion true,
but premises don't support the conclusion.
You are reading this book.
This book was printed in the U.S.
Therefore, this book costs less than $20.

Premises support the conclusion,
but one of the premises is false.
You are reading this book.
Everyone who reads this book is a man.
So you are a man.

If one of the premises is dubious or false, then we have no reason to accept the conclusion. From a false premise we can derive both true claims and false claims. ***An argument is no better than its least plausible premise.***

False premise, true conclusion.
Lassie is a cat.
All cats have fur.
So Lassie has fur.

False premise, false conclusion.
Lassie is a dog.
All dogs can fly.
So Lassie can fly.

4 Evaluating Premises

We need to establish criteria for when we
should accept the premises of an argument.

Three Attitudes We Can Take to the Truth of a Claim
- Accept the claim as true.
- Reject the claim as false.
- Suspend judgment.

---

not believe ≠ believe is false
lack of evidence ≠ evidence it is false

1. *Our most reliable source of information about the world
is our own experience.*

But claims based on our own experience are no better
than our memory and the functioning of our senses at the
time of the experience. We reject or don't accept a claim
about our own experience if:

- We have good reason to doubt our memory.
- The claim contradicts other experiences of ours, and
  there is a good argument (theory) against the claim.

The world is flat.
Reject our experience. There is a good theory against the claim.

My date was gone from the room for over an hour at the party.
Suspend judgment? If you were drunk, don't accept this.

A claim may seem to be about your own experience, yet
it is really a conclusion drawn from your experience.

If you meet two Japanese students who are good at math, you're justified in claiming "Two Japanese students are good at math," not "All Japanese students are good at math."

2. We can accept claims that are made by someone we know and trust and who is an authority about that kind of claim.

Zoe tells Harry to stay away from the area of town around S. 3rd. She's seen people doing drugs there and knows two people who have been held up in that neighborhood. Zoe is reliable, and her knowledge would matter about these claims.

Tom's mother tells him that he should major in business so he can get ahead in life. Should he believe her? She can tell him about her friends' children. But what are the chances of getting a good job with a degree in business? It would be better to check at the local colleges where they keep records on hiring graduates. He shouldn't reject her claim; he should suspend judgment until he gets more information.

3. We can accept claims that are made by a reputable authority whom we can trust as an expert on this kind of claim and who has no motive to mislead.

The Surgeon General announces that smoking is bad for your health. He's got no axe to grind. He's a physician. He's in a position to survey the research on the subject. Believe him.

But the doctor hired by the tobacco company says there's no proof that smoking is addictive or causes lung cancer. Is he an expert on smoking-related diseases? Or perhaps an allergist or pediatrician? It matters for whether to trust his ability to interpret the data. And he has a motive to mislead. There's no reason to accept his claim, and some motive for rejecting it.

The new Surgeon General says that marijuana should be legal. What kind of authority is she on this subject? Is she a politician? A lawyer? What kind of expertise does she have on matters of law and public policy? She is an authority figure, but not an expert on *this* kind of claim. No reason to accept it.

4. We can accept a claim put forward in a reputable journal or reference source.

The New England Journal of Medicine is regularly quoted in newspapers, and for good reason. The articles in it are subjected to peer review: Experts in the subject are asked to evaluate whether the research was done to scientific standards.

The National Geographic has less reliable standards, since they pay for their own research in order to sell their magazine. But it's pretty reliable about natural history and ethnography.

What about the *Dictionary of Biography*? There's probably no motive for bias in it, though it may be incomplete. Yet it's often hard to get a better source of information about, say, a 19th century physician.

On the other hand, anyone can incorporate into a nonprofit corporation called "The Advanced Reasoning Forum," or any other title you like. A name is not enough to go by.

5. *We can accept a claim from a media source that is usually reliable and has no obvious motive to mislead.*

With newspapers, television, radio, magazines, and other media sources it's partly like trusting your friend and partly like trusting an authority. The more you read a particular newspaper, the better you'll be able to judge whether to trust its news gathering as reliable. The more you read a particular magazine, the better you'll be able to judge whether there's an editorial bias.

Some factors you can use to evaluate a news report:
• The source has been reliable in the past.
• The source doesn't have a bias on the topic.
• The source being quoted is named.

There's never good reason to accept a claim from an unnamed source.

A television network consistently gives a bias against a particular presidential candidate. So when it says that the candidate contradicted himself twice yesterday, you should take it with a grain of salt. That may be true, but it may be a matter of interpretation. Or it may be plain false.

"Usually reliable sources" are not even as reliable as the person who is quoting them; anyway they've covered themselves by saying "usually."

Arguing backwards Believing the premises because the conclusion is true. *An argument is supposed to convince us that its conclusion is true, not that its premises are true.*

All dogs bark.
Spot is a dog.
So Spot barks.

The conclusion is true. And the premises are reasonable. So it's a good argument? No. In Africa there are two breeds of dogs that don't bark. The first premise isn't true, and the argument is bad.

Plausibility isn't truth. Learn when to *suspend judgment.* There are no absolute rules for when we should accept, when reject, and when suspend judgment about a claim. It's a skill, weighing up the following in order of importance:

Reject:	The claim contradicts personal experience. (Exceptions: Our memory is not good; there's a good argument against our understanding of our experience; it's not our experience at all, but what we've concluded from it.)
Accept:	The claim is known by personal experience.
Reject:	The claim contradicts other claims we know to be true.
Reject:	Two claims used as premises contradict each other.
Accept:	The claim is made by someone whom we know and trust and who is an authority about that kind of claim.
Accept:	The claim is offered by a reputable authority whom we can trust as an expert about this kind of claim and who has no motive to mislead.
Accept:	The claim is put forward in a reputable journal or reference source.
Accept:	The claim is in a media source that's usually reliable and has no obvious motive to mislead.

Here are some common mistakes in applying these criteria, *if* the generic premise is false.

Appeal to authority   A bad argument that uses or requires as premise:

"(Almost) anything that _____ says about ____ is true."

— What do you think of the new seat belt law?
— It must be bad, 'cause William Buckley said so.

Mistaking the person for the claim   A bad argument that uses or requires as premise:

"(Almost) anything that _____ says about ____ is false."

Mistaking the person for the argument   A bad argument that uses or requires as premise:

"(Almost) any argument that _____ gives about ____ is bad."

Zoe: I went to Professor Zzzyzzx's talk about writing last night. He said that the best way to start on a novel is to make an outline of the plot.
Suzy: Are you kidding? He can't even speak English.

Appeal to common practice   A bad argument that uses or requires as premise:

"If (almost) everyone else (in this group) does it, then it's O.K. to do."

— You shouldn't stay out so late. It's dangerous, so I want you home early.
— But none of my friends have curfews and they stay out as long as they want.

Appeal to common belief   An argument that uses or requires as premise:

"If (almost) everyone else (in this group) believes it, then it's true."

Phony refutation   An argument that uses or requires as premises both:

" ____ has done or said ____, which shows that he or she does not believe the conclusion of his or her own argument" *and* "If someone does not believe the conclusion of his or her own argument, then the argument is bad."

— We should stop logging old-growth forests. There are very few of them left in the U.S. They are important watersheds and preserve wildlife. And once cut, we cannot recreate them.
— You say we should stop logging old-growth forests? Who are you kidding? You just built a log cabin on the mountain.

— We should tax cigarettes much more heavily. It will stop kids from starting to smoke.
— I can't believe you said that. Don't you smoke three packs a day?

Whether an argument is good or bad does not depend on who made it.

But remember, these are bad ways to evaluate claims only if the generic premise is false.

You go to England and everyone else is driving on the left-hand side. It's not wrong to conclude that you should, too.

The American Medical Association tells us "Smoking can cause cancer." The group is composed of reliable experts, so perhaps you should accept their claim.

"I can't solve this math question. It's too hard for a high school student. But my math teacher says the answer is 3. So the answer must be 3." This is a reliable authority.

And above all, personal experience is your best guide. Don't trust others more than yourself about what you know best.

— I played doubles on my team for four years. It is definitely a more intense game than playing singles.
— Yesterday on the news Michael Chang said that doubles in tennis is much easier because there are two people covering almost the same playing area.
— I guess he must be right then.

5 The Conclusion Follows

The conclusion follows from the premises
means that the argument is valid or strong.

Valid Argument   An argument for which it is impossible
for the premises to be true and the conclusion false (at the
same time). An argument is *invalid* if it is not valid.

Strong and Weak Arguments   We classify invalid arguments on a scale from very strong to weak. An argument
is *very strong* if it is almost impossible for the premises
to be true and the conclusion false (at the same time).
An argument is *weak* if it is likely that the premises could
be true and conclusion false (at the same time).

Either an argument is valid or it isn't. There are no degrees
to it. But whether an argument is strong is a matter of degree.

All dogs bark.
Ralph is a dog.
Therefore, Ralph barks.

Valid. Impossible for the premises to be true and conclusion false
at the same time.

All parakeets anyone I know has ever seen or heard or read about
are under 2' tall. Therefore, the parakeets on sale at Boulevard
Mall are under 2' tall.

Strong. Surveying all the ways the premise could be true, we think
that yes, a new supergrow bird food could have been formulated and
the parakeets at the local mall are really 2´ tall, we just haven't

17

heard about it. Or a rare giant parakeet from the Amazon forest could have been discovered and brought here. Or a UFO might have abducted a parakeet by mistake, hit it with growing rays, and the bird is gigantic. So the argument is not valid. But all these ways the premise could be true and conclusion false are *so very unlikely,* almost preposterous, that we would have very good reason to believe the conclusion if the premise is true, even though the conclusion might be false.

Good teachers give fair exams. Dr. E gives fair exams. So Dr. E is a good teacher.

Weak. Dr. E might bore his students to tears and just copy good exams from the instructor's manual. Or he might get good exams from another teacher. There are lots of possibilities that are not preposterous.

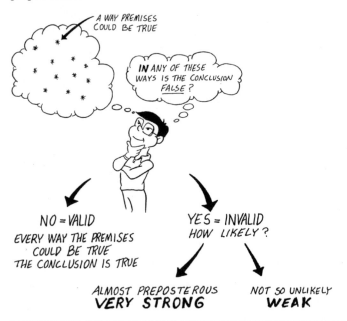

> How do we show that an argument is not valid or is weak?
> *We give an example, a possible way in which the premises could be true and conclusion false.*
> To reason well you must use your *imagination.*

For an argument to be good, there must be good reason to believe the premises (the premises are plausible) and the conclusion must follow from the premises.

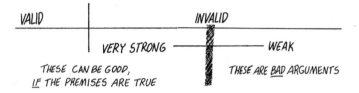

Note:
* Only invalid arguments are classified from strong to weak.
* Every weak argument is bad.
* Not every valid or strong argument is good.

Since an argument is intended to convince, for it to be good the premises must be more plausible than the conclusion. An argument *begs the question* if its premises are no more plausible than its conclusion.

Dogs have souls.
Therefore, you should treat dogs humanely.

— God exists.
— How do you know?
— 'Cause the Bible says so.
— But why do you think that's true?
— 'Cause God wrote the Bible.

Tests for an Argument to be Good
* The premises are plausible.
* The argument is valid or strong.
* The premises are more plausible than the conclusion.

Dr. E is a philosophy professor. All philosophy professors prefer dogs to cats. So Dr. E prefers dogs to cats.
Valid, but bad. One of the premises is false.

Dick is a bachelor. So Dick was never married.
Weak, bad. Dick could have been divorced.

Mary Ellen's hair is naturally brown. Today Mary Ellen's hair is red. So she dyed her hair.
Strong, good if the premises are true. Mary Ellen might be taking a new medication that has a strong effect. Or she might have been too close to her car when they were painting it, or . . . The possible ways in which the premises could be true and conclusion false all seem preposterous.

Prosecuting attorney: The defendant intended to kill Louise. He bought a gun three days before he shot her. He practiced shooting at a target that had her name written across it. He staked out her home for two nights. He shot her twice.
Strong, good if the premises are true.

Defendant: I didn't mean to kill Louise. I only wanted to scare her. That's what was in my mind. Only that, I swear.
Weak, bad. All he is saying may be true, yet the argument is weak, and we have no good reason to believe the conclusion. What he says wouldn't create reasonable doubt.

— Today's the 29th, right?
— No, it's the first.
— The first?
— Yes, yesterday was the 28th of February, and February has just 28 days. Only in years divisible by four does it have 29 days.
Valid, good. The premises were true (it doesn't say that in all years divisible by four February has 29 days).

Whenever Spot barks, there's a cat outside. Since he's barking now, there must be a cat outside.
Valid, but bad. The possibility that he may be barking at the garbageman doesn't show that the argument is weak—it shows that the first premise is false.

If the conclusion of a valid argument is false,
one of the premises must be false.

6 Repairing Arguments

Many arguments we encounter daily are not valid
or strong as stated, yet they really aren't bad.

— I heard that Wanda has a pet.
— It must be a dog, because I heard barking in her house
yesterday. And I know she doesn't let people bring their
pets over to her home.

This is missing a premise to be a good argument: "Almost any pet
that barks is a dog." But why bother saying that? Everyone knows
it, and the argument is good enough without it.

In order to evaluate arguments, we need to make some
assumptions about the people with whom we reason.

Rationality and Arguments If you recognize that
an argument is good, then it is irrational to believe
the conclusion is false.

What if you hear an argument for both sides, and you can't
find a flaw in either? Then you should *suspend judgment* on
whether the claim is true until you can investigate more.

The Principle of Rational Discussion We assume that
the other person who is discussing with us or whose
arguments we are evaluating:
1. Knows about the subject under discussion.
2. Is able and willing to reason well.
3. Is not lying.

What justification do we have for invoking this principle? Not everyone fits these criteria all the time. But if people don't satisfy the Principle of Rational Discussion, there's no point in reasoning with them.

- If they don't know about the subject, educate, don't debate.
- If they aren't able to reason well, teach them.
- If they aren't willing to reason well, walk away.
- If they're lying, then the only point of reasoning with them is to catch them out in their lies.

Still many people don't follow the Principle of Rational Discussion. They don't care if your argument is good. Why not use bad methods of persuasion? Why should we follow these rules and assume them of others? If you don't:

- You are denying the essentials of democracy.
- You are likely to undermine your own ability to evaluate arguments.
- You are not as likely to convince others.

> If you once forfeit the confidence of your fellow citizens, you can never regain their respect and esteem. It is true that you may fool all the people some of the time; you can even fool some of the people all the time; but you can't fool all of the people all the time.
> Abraham Lincoln

With the Principle of Rational Discussion, we can formulate a guide to help us in evaluating arguments. Since the person is supposed to be able to reason well, we can add a premise only if it makes the argument stronger or valid and doesn't beg the question. Since the person isn't lying and knows the subject under discussion, any premise we add should be plausible, and plausible to the other person. Further, we can delete a premise if that doesn't make the argument any weaker.

A premise is *irrelevant* if you can delete it and the argument isn't any weaker.

> ### *The Guide to Repairing Arguments* Given an (implicit) argument that is apparently defective, we are justified in *adding* a premise or conclusion if it satisfies all three of:
>
> 1. The argument becomes stronger or valid.
> 2. The premise is plausible and would seem plausible to the other person.
> 3. The premise is more plausible than the conclusion.
>
> If the argument is then valid or strong, yet one of the original premises is false or dubious, we may *delete* that premise if the argument remains valid or strong.

We don't need to know what the speaker was thinking in order to find a claim that makes the argument strong or valid, so we take (1) to have priority over (2). By first trying to make the argument valid or strong, we show the other person what he or she needs to assume to make the argument good.

> ### *Unrepairable Arguments* We can't repair an argument if any one of the following hold:
> - There's no argument there.
> - The argument is so lacking in coherence that there's nothing obvious to add.
> - The premises it uses are false or very dubious and cannot be deleted.
> - The obvious premise to add would make the argument weak.
> - The obvious premise to add to make the argument strong or valid is false.
> - The conclusion is clearly false.

When you show that an argument is bad,
you haven't proved that the conclusion is false.

1. No dog meows. So Juney does not meow.

Evaluation "Juney is a dog" is the only premise that will make this a valid or strong argument. So we add that. Then, if this new claim is true, the argument is good.

   We don't add "Juney barks." That's true and may seem obvious to the person who stated the argument, but it doesn't make the argument any better. So adding it violates (1) of the Guide. We repair only as needed.

2. All dogs bark. So Ralph is a dog.

Evaluation The obvious premise to add is "Ralph barks." But that makes the argument weak (Ralph could be a seal, or a fox, or . . .). The argument is unrepairable, and hence bad.

3. Dr. E is a good teacher, because he gives fair exams.

Evaluation The unstated premise needed here is "Almost any teacher who gives fair exams is a good teacher." That gives a strong argument. But it's very dubious, since a teacher could copy fair exams from the instructor's manual. (If you thought the claim that's needed is "Good teachers give fair exams," reread the example on p. 18.) The argument can't be repaired because the obvious premise to add to make the argument strong or valid is false or dubious.

   But can't we make it strong by adding, say, "Dr. E gives great explanations," "Dr. E is amusing," "Dr. E never misses class," . . .? Yes, all those are true, and perhaps obvious to the person. But adding those doesn't repair this argument—it makes a whole new argument.

   Don't put words in someone's mouth.

4. Tom's instructor teaches critical thinking. Tom has to pay tuition for that course. Therefore, Tom will get a passing grade in critical thinking.

Evaluation The argument is weak—and it *is* an argument: The word "therefore" tells us that. But there's no obvious way to repair it. The person apparently can't reason. It's unrepairable, and hence bad.

5. You shouldn't eat the fat on your steak. Haven't you heard that cholesterol is bad for you?

Evaluation The conclusion is the first sentence. But what are the premises? The speaker's question is rhetorical, meant to be taken as an assertion: "Cholesterol is bad for you." But that alone won't give us the conclusion. We need something like "Steak fat has a lot of cholesterol" and "You shouldn't eat anything that's bad for you." Premises like these are so obvious we don't bother to say them. The argument is O.K.

6. You're going to vote for the Socialist Party candidate for President? Don't you realize that means your vote will be wasted?

Evaluation Here, too, the questions are rhetorical, meant to be taken as assertions: "Don't vote for the Socialist Party candidate" (the conclusion) and "Your vote will be wasted" (the premise). This sounds reasonable, though something is missing. A visitor from Denmark may not know "The Socialist Party candidate doesn't have a chance of winning." But she may also question why that matters. We'd have to fill in the argument further: "If you vote for someone who doesn't have a chance of winning, then your vote will be wasted." And when we add that premise we see the argument that used such "obvious" premises is really not very good. Why should we believe that if you vote for someone who doesn't stand a chance of winning then your vote is wasted? If that were true, then who wins is the only important result of an election, rather than, say, making a position understood by the electorate. At best we can say that when the unstated premises are added in, we get an argument one of whose premises needs a substantial argument to convince us that it is true.

7. Cats are more likely than dogs to carry diseases harmful to humans. Cats kill songbirds and can kill people's pets. Cats disturb people at night with their screeching and clattering in garbage cans. Cats leave pawprints on cars and will sleep in unattended cars. Cats are not as pleasant as dogs and are owned only by people who have satanic affinities. So there should be a leash law for cats just as much as for dogs.

Evaluation This letter to the editor is going pretty well until the next to last sentence. That claim is a bit dubious, and the argument would be just as strong without it. So we should delete it. Then we have an argument which, with some unstated premises you can supply, is pretty good.

8. Harry's new dog is a pit bull. So it must be dangerous.

Evaluation The question here is whether we should try to make this argument valid or strong. The word "must" strongly suggests that the speaker thinks the argument he's making is valid. Unless we have good reason to think otherwise, "must" and "have to" will signal to us that we should repair the argument as valid.

But then the only premise we could add is "All pit bulls are dangerous." And that's false. So the argument is unrepairable.

9.   In a famous speech, Martin Luther King Jr. said:

I have a dream that one day this nation will rise up and live out the true meaning of its creed: "We hold these truths to be self-evident—that all men are created equal." . . . I have a dream that one day even the state of Mississippi, a desert state sweltering with the heat of injustice and oppression, will be transformed into an oasis of freedom and justice. I have a dream that my four little children will one day live in a nation where they will not be judged by the color of their skin but by the content of their character. [Quoted from *Let the Trumpet Sound,* by Stephen B. Oates.]

. . . King is also presenting a logical argument . . . the argument might be stated as follows; "America was founded on the principle that all men are created equal. This implies that people should not be judged by skin color, which is an accident of birth, but rather by what they make of themselves ('the content of their character'). To be consistent with this principle, America should treat black people and white people alike."

The Art of Reasoning, David Kelley

Evaluation The rewriting of this passage is too much of a stretch—putting words in someone's mouth—to be appropriate. Where did David Kelley get the premise "This implies . . ."? Stating my dreams and hoping others will share them is not an argument. Martin Luther King, Jr. knew how to argue well and could do so when he wanted. We're not going to make his words more respectable by pretending they're an argument. Not every good attempt to persuade is an argument.

10. Environmentalists should not be allowed to tell us what to do. The federal government should not be allowed to tell us what to do. Therefore, we should go ahead and allow logging in old-growth forests.

Evaluation The speaker has confused whether we have the right to cut down forests with whether we should cut them down. The argument is weak; indeed, we could delete either premise and it wouldn't be any weaker. That is, the speaker's assumptions are irrelevant (p. 22) to the conclusion.

When someone leaves a conclusion unsaid, he is *implying* the conclusion. When you decide that an unstated claim is the conclusion, you are *inferring* that claim. We can also say that someone is implying a claim if in context it's clear that he believes the claim. In that case we infer that the person believes the claim.

I'm not going to vote, because no matter who is president nothing is going to get done about violence in the schools.
Evaluation An unstated claim is needed to make sense of what is said: "If no matter who is president nothing is going to get done about violence in the schools, then you shouldn't vote for president." We infer this from the person's remarks; he has implied it.

Instructor: My best students hand in extra-credit work.
Evaluation You might think the instructor is implying that you need to do extra-credit work to do well in the course. But she could say that you inferred incorrectly: She was just making an observation.

Instructor: You look terrific in that new outfit.
Evaluation: Is this sexual harassment? Be careful what you infer.

7 Compound Claims

> A *compound claim* is one that is composed of other claims, but has to be viewed as just one claim.

Either a Democrat will win the election or a Republican will win the election. *Compound.*

Either a Democrat or a Republican will win the election. *Compound.* (Rewrite this as the previous one.)

Columbus landed in South Carolina or on some island near there. *Compound.*

If Dick was working today, then Maria called in sick. *Compound.*

Suzy will pass her exam because she studied so hard. *Not compound.* This is an argument ("because" is an indicator).

Alternatives   Claims that are parts of an "or" claim.

Conditional Claim   A claim that is or can be rewritten as an "if . . . then . . ." claim that must have the same truth-value.

Antecedent and Consequent   In a conditional (rewritten as) "If A, then B", the claim A is the *antecedent,* the claim B is the *consequent.*

Dick or Zoe will go to the grocery to get eggs.
An "or" claim. Alternatives: "Dick will go to the grocery to get eggs"; "Zoe will go the grocery to get eggs."

If Spot ran away, then the gate was left open.
Conditional. Antecedent: "Spot ran away". Consequent: "The gate was left open."

I'll never talk to you again if you don't apologize.

Conditional. Antecedent: "You don't apologize." Consequent: "I'll never talk to you again."

Bring me an ice cream cone and I'll be happy.

Conditional. Antecedent: "You bring me an ice cream cone." Consequent: "I'll be happy."

Loving someone means you never throw dishes at them.

Conditional. Antecedent: "You love someone." Consequent: "You never throw dishes at them."

Maria will not get AIDS since she is celibate now.

Not a conditional. Perhaps an argument, with "since" introducing a premise.

If Dick goes to the basketball game, then either he got a free ticket or he borrowed money for one.

Conditional. Antecedent: "Dick goes to the basketball game." Consequent: (another compound claim) "Dick got a free ticket or he borrowed money for one."

> **Contradictory of a Claim**   A *contradictory* of a claim is one that always has the opposite truth-value.

Spot barks.

Contradictory: Spot does not bark.

Dick isn't a student.

Contradictory: Dick is a student. (A contradictory needn't have "not" in it.)

Suzy will go to the movies or she will stay home.

Contradictory: Suzy won't go to the movies and she won't stay home.

Tom or Suzy will pick up Manuel for class today.

Contradictory: Neither Tom nor Suzy will pick up Manuel for class today.

> ### Contradictory of an "or" Claim
> A or B *has contradictory* not A and not B.
>
> ### Contradictory of a Conditional
> If A, then B *has contradictory* A, but not B.

The contradictory of a conditional is NOT another conditional. For example:

† If Suzy studies three hours every day, she will pass biology.

Contradictory: Suzy studies three hours every day *and* she will *not* pass biology.
(Colloquially we usually use "but" instead of "and".)

Not contradictory: If Suzy doesn't study three hours every day, she won't pass biology. (Both this and † could be true.)

Not contradictory: If Suzy doesn't study three hours every day, she will pass biology. (Both this and † could be true: the biology teacher might just decide to pass everyone.)

Not contradictory: If Suzy studies three hours every day, she will not pass biology. (Both this and † could be true by default if Suzy just doesn't study.)

If Spot barks, then Flo's cat will run away.
Contradictory: Spot barked, but Flo's cat did not run away.

If Spot got out of the yard, then he was chasing a squirrel.
Contradictory: Spot got out of the yard, but he wasn't chasing a squirrel.

If cats had no fur, they would still give people allergies.
Contradictory: Even if cats had no fur, still give people allergies.
"Even if" is often used instead of "but". It functions just as "although" or "despite that". The "if" in it does not create a conditional.

Bring me an ice cream cone and I'll be happy.
Contradictory: Despite that you brought me an ice cream cone, I'm not happy.

Here are some correct and incorrect ways to reason with compound claims. We use "A" and "B" to stand for any claims, and a diagram with arrow to indicate "therefore".

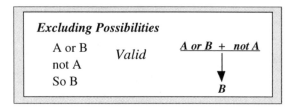

Either there is a wheelchair ramp at the school dance, or Manuel stayed home. But there isn't a wheelchair ramp at the school dance. Therefore, Manuel stayed home.

Or there can be are more alternatives:

$$A \text{ or } B \text{ or } C \quad + \quad not\, A \quad + \quad not\, B$$
$$\downarrow$$
$$C$$

Or we can exclude just some of the possibilities:

Either all criminals should be locked up forever, or we should put more money into rehabilitating criminals, or we should accept that our streets will never be safe, or we should have some system for monitoring ex-convicts. (*This is all one claim*: A or B or C or D.) We can't lock up all criminals forever, because it would be too expensive. We definitely won't accept that our streets will never be safe. So either we should put more money into rehabilitating criminals, or we should have some system for monitoring ex-convicts.

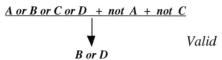

Valid

False dilemma A bad use of excluding possibilities, where the "or" claim is false or implausible.

— Look at these bills, you're either going to have to get rid

of those nasty expensive cigars or get rid of Spot.
— What are you talking about? We can't get rid of Spot.
— So you agree, you'll give up smoking those cigars.
False dilemma. They could economize on dining out.

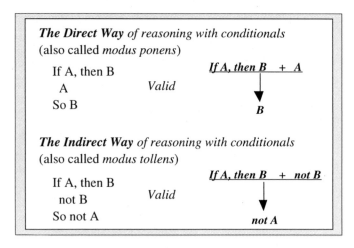

Here "not B" stands for "the contradictory of B."

If Spot barks, then Dick will wake up.
Spot barked.
So Dick woke up.
Valid, the direct way.

If Spot barks, then Dick will wake up.
Dick didn't wake up.
So Spot didn't bark.
Valid, the indirect way.

If Suzy doesn't call early, then Zoe won't go shopping.
Zoe went shopping.
So Suzy called early.
Valid, the indirect way. The contradictory doesn't use "not".

Zoe won't go shopping if Dick comes home early.
Zoe went shopping.
So Dick didn't come home early.
Valid, the indirect way.

If Flo comes over to play,

If it's the day for the garbageman,

Then Dick will wake up.

If Suzy calls early,

If Spot barks,

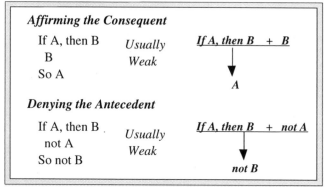

Affirming the Consequent

If A, then B	*Usually*	*If A, then B* + B
B	*Weak*	
So A		A

Denying the Antecedent

If A, then B	*Usually*	*If A, then B* + *not A*
not A	*Weak*	
So not B		*not B*

If Spot barks, then Dick will wake up.
Dick woke up.
So Spot barked.

Affirming the consequent. This is weak. Maybe Suzy called, or

Flo came over to play. It's *reasoning backwards.*

If it's the day for the garbageman, then Dick will wake up.
It's not the day for the garbageman.
So Dick didn't wake up.

Denying the antecedent. Even though the garbageman didn't come, maybe Spot barked or Suzy called early. You can't overlook other possibilities. This, too, is reasoning backwards.

If Maria doesn't call Manuel, then Manuel will miss his class.
Maria did call Manuel.
So Manuel didn't miss his class.

Affirming the consequent. The "not" in the form indicates a contradictory.

> *If* Maria doesn't call Manuel, *then* Manuel will miss his class.
>   A   B
>
> Maria did call Manuel.   *So* Manuel didn't miss his class.
>   not A   not B

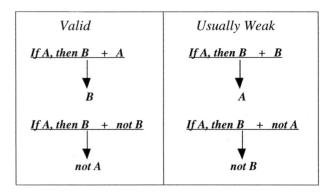

Valid	*Usually Weak*
If A, then B + *A*	*If A, then B* + *B*
↓	↓
B	*A*
If A, then B + *not B*	*If A, then B* + *not A*
↓	↓
not A	*not B*

    These invalid forms of arguing are obvious confusions with valid forms, mistakes a good reasoner doesn't make. When you see one, *don't bother to repair the argument.*

If Suzy called early, then Dick woke up.
So Dick didn't wake up.

Evaluation The obvious premise to add is "Suzy didn't call early." But that makes the argument weak, so the argument is unrepairable.

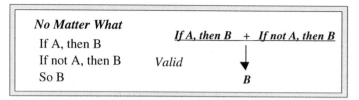

No Matter What
If A, then B
If not A, then B
So B

Valid

If A, then B + *If not A, then B*

B

Dick: If I study for my math exam this weekend we won't be able to have a good time at the beach.

Zoe: But if you don't study for your exam, you'll worry about it like you always do, and we won't have a good time at the beach. So it looks like this weekend is shot.

Contrapositive The *contrapositive* of "If A, then B" is "If not B, then not A." The contrapositive is true exactly when the original conditional is true.

If Spot barks, then Dick will wake up.

Contrapositive: If Dick doesn't wake up, then Spot didn't bark. (See the picture on p. 33.)

A only if B *can be replaced by* If A, then B.

All the following have the same truth-value:

If you get a speeding ticket, you went over the speed limit.

You can get a speeding ticket *only if* you are going over the speed limit.

If you don't go over the speed limit, then you won't get a speeding ticket. (*Contrapositive*)

Do not confuse "only if" with "if":

Zoe: I'll go hiking with you only if you'll go to this Jane Austen movie with me.

Dick: O.K., I'll go to the movie.

(A week later, after Dick's gone to a Jane Austen movie with Zoe)

Zoe: I'm not going to go hiking with you. You ruined my dinner party.

Evaluation Zoe didn't go back on her word. Zoe said she'd go only if Dick went to the movie, not if he went to the movie.

> "If A, then B" is always true
>
> means   A is *sufficient* for B
>   B is *necessary* for A

(See the picture on p. 33.)

Flo coming over early is sufficient for Dick to wake up.

Zoe being noisy making breakfast is sufficient to get Dick to wake up.

Dick waking up is necessary (required, inevitable) when Zoe is noisy.

Dick waking up is necessary (required, inevitable) when Spot barks.

Do not confuse necessary and sufficient conditions.

Manuel: It's wrong that Betty didn't make the basketball team.

Lee: Yeah. I watched the tryouts and she was great. She hit a couple three-pointers, and she can really jump.

Manuel: And the coach chose only girls who could jump well and hit three-pointers.

Lee: She had everything you need to get on the team.

Evaluation Lee has mistaken a necessary condition for a sufficient condition: "only" is used as in "only if".

Reasoning in a chain is important. We go by little steps: if A, then B; if B, then C; . . . Then if A is true, we can conclude the very last consequent.

If Dick takes Spot for a walk, then Zoe will cook dinner.
And if Zoe cooks dinner, then Dick will do the dishes.
So if Dick takes Spot for a walk, then he'll do the dishes.
But Dick did take Spot for a walk. So he must've done the dishes.

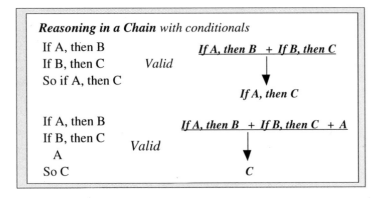

Slippery slope A bad argument that uses a chain of conditionals, some or many of which are false or dubious.

Don't get a credit card! If you do, you'll be tempted to spend money you don't have. Then you'll max out on your card. Then you'll be in real debt. And you'll have to drop out of school to pay your bills. You'll end up a failure in life.

Slippery slope. Rewrite it using "if . . . then . . .".

Reasoning from Hypotheses If you start with an assumption or hypothesis A that you don't know to be true and make a good argument for B, then what you have established is "If A, then B."

Lee: I'm thinking of majoring in biology.

Maria: That means you'll take summer school. Here's why: You're in your second year now. To finish in four years like you told me you need to, you'll have to take all the upper-division biology courses your last two years. And you can't take any of those until you've finished the three-semester calculus course. So you'll have to take calculus over the summer in order to finish in four years.

Maria has not proved that Lee has to go to summer school. Rather, on the assumption (hypothesis) that Lee will major in biology, Lee will have to go to summer school. That is, Maria has proved: If Lee majors in biology, then he'll have to go to summer school.

8 Counterarguments

Raising objections and answering them
is part of making good arguments.

Dick: Zoe, we ought to get another dog.
Zoe: What's wrong with Spot?
Dick: Oh, no, I mean to keep Spot company.
Zoe: Spot has us. He doesn't need company.
Dick: But we're gone a lot. And he's always escaping from the
      yard, 'cause he's lonely. And we don't give him enough
      time. He should be out running around more.
Zoe: But think of all the work! We'll have to feed the new dog.
      And think of all the time necessary to train it.
Dick: I'll train him. We can feed him at the same time as Spot,
      and dog food is cheap. It won't cost much.

Dick is trying to convince Zoe to believe, "We should
get another dog." But he has to answer her objections.

We ought to get another dog.
   (*objection*) We already have Spot.
The other dog will keep Spot company. (*answer*)
   (*objection*) Spot already has us for company.
We are gone a lot. (*answer*)
He is always escaping from the yard. (*answer*)
He's lonely. (*answer*)
We don't give him enough time. (*answer*)
He should be out running around more. (*answer*)
   (*objection*) It will be a lot of work to have a new dog.
   (*objection*) We will have to feed the new dog.
   (*objection*) It will take a lot of time to train the new dog.
Dick will train him. (*answer*)

We can feed him at the same time as Spot. (*answer*)

Dog food is cheap. (*answer*)

Argument. Counterargument. Counter-counterargument. Objections are raised: Someone puts forward a claim that, if true, makes one of our claims false or at least doubtful. We then have to answer that challenge to sustain our argument. *Knocking off an objection is a mini-argument within your argument—if it's not a good (though brief) argument, it won't do the job.*

Or you could say, "I hadn't thought of that. I guess you're right." *Or* you could say, "I don't know. I'll have to think about that."

In making an argument, you'll want to make it strong. You might think you have a great one. All the premises seem obvious and they glue together to get the conclusion. But if you imagine someone objecting, you can see how to give better support for doubtful premises. And answering counterarguments in your own writing allows the reader to see you haven't ignored some obvious objections. All you have to do is make a list of the pros and cons. Then answer the other side.

Direct Ways of Refuting an Argument

1. Show that at least one of the premises is false.
2. Show that the argument isn't valid or strong.
3. Show that the conclusion is false.

It's useless to kill flies. The ones you kill will be the slowest, because the fastest ones will evade you. So you will be killing off the slowest ones, and the fastest ones will remain. Over time, then, the genes for being fast will predominate. Then with super-fast flies, it will be impossible to kill them anyway. So it's useless to kill flies.

To refute this argument: We might object to one of the premises, saying that you won't be killing the slowest ones, but only the ones that happen to come into your house.

Or we might agree with the premises, but note that "over time" could be thousands of years, so the conclusion doesn't follow.

Or we could attack the conclusion directly, pointing out that we kill flies all the time and it keeps the house clean.

Reducing to the Absurd   To *reduce to the absurd* is to show that at least one of several claims is false or dubious, or collectively they are unacceptable, by drawing a false or unwanted conclusion from them.

You complain that taxes are already too high and there is too much crime. And you say we should permanently lock up everyone who has been convicted of three felonies. In the places where this has been instituted it hasn't reduced the crime rate. So we will have many, many more people who will be incarcerated for their entire lives. We will need more prisons, many more, because these people will be in forever. We will need to employ more guards. We will need to pay for a lot of health-care for these people when they are elderly. Thus, if you lock up everyone who has been convicted of three felonies, we will have to pay substantially higher taxes. Since you are adamant that taxes are too high and crime is too prevalent, you should abandon your claim that we should permanently lock up everyone who has been convicted of three felonies.

Reducing to the absurd is an indirect way to refute an argument. If a valid or strong argument has a false conclusion, then one of the (unstated) premises is implausible.

Beware: Be sure the argument you use to get the false or absurd conclusion is strong or valid and doesn't use any other dubious claims. Only then do you have good reason to believe there's a problem with the original set of claims.

One way to reduce to the absurd is to use similar

premises in an argument that sounds just like the original, yet leads to an absurd conclusion. This is refuting by analogy (see Chapter 10).

Look, your argument against killing flies is bad. We could use the same argument against killing bacteria, or against killing chickens for dinner from a farmer's henhouse. Those conclusions would be absurd.

Attempts to refute that are bad arguments:

Phony refutations (pp. 15–16)

Slippery slope (p. 37)

Ridicule

Dr. E: I hear that your department elected a woman as chairman.
Professor Zzzyzzx: Jah, jah, dat is right. Und now ve is trying to
decide vat we should be calling her—"chairman" or
"chairwoman" or "chairperson."
Dr. E: "Chairperson"? Why not use a neutral term that's really
appropriate for the position, like "chaircreature"?

No argument has been given for why "chairman" shouldn't be replaced by "chairperson," although Dr. E thinks he's shown that the idea is absurd. In rational discussion, ridicule is a device to end arguments, belittle your opponent, and make enemies.

Strawman   A bad way to refute an argument by putting words in your opponent's mouth.

Tom: Unless we allow the logging of old-growth forests in
this county, we'll lose the timber industry and these
towns will die.
Dick: So you're saying that you don't care what happens to
the spotted owl and to our rivers and the water we
drink?
Tom: I said nothing of the sort. You've misrepresented my
position.

The only reasonable response to a straw man is to say calmly that that isn't what you said.

9   General Claims

We need to know how to reason with claims
that are asserted about all, or some, or a few,
or no things.

All means "Every single one, no exceptions."
Sometimes *all* is meant as "Every single one,
and there is at least one." Which reading is best
may depend on the argument.

Some means "At least one." Sometimes *some*
is meant as "At least one, but not all." Which
reading is best may depend on the argument.

All dogs are mammals. *True.*

All dogs bark. *False–*on either reading of "all".

All polar bears in Antarctica can swim.
*True–*if you understand "all" as every single one. *False–*if you
understand "all" to mean as well "at least one", since there aren't
any polar bears in Antarctica.

Some dogs bark. *True–*on either reading of "some".

Some dogs are mammals.
*True–*if you understand "some" to mean just "at least one".
*False–*if you understand "some" to mean as well "and not all".

Universal Claim   A claim that can be rewritten
as an "all" claim that must have the same truth-value.

Existential Claim   A claim that can be rewritten
as a "some" claim that must have the same truth-value.

42

The following universal claims all have the same truth-value:

All dogs bark.   Dogs bark.
Every dog barks.   Everything that's a dog barks.

The following existential claims all have the same truth-value:

Some dogs can't bark.   At least one dog can't bark.
There is a dog that can't bark. There exists a dog that can't bark.

> ***Negative Universal Claim*** A claim that can be
> rewritten as a "no" claim or an "all not" claim that
> must have the same truth-value.

The following negative universal claims have the same truth-value:

No dog likes cats.   Nothing that's a dog likes cats.
All dogs do not like cats.   Not even one dog likes cats.

> *Only* S are P   means   All P are S.

Only dogs bark.
Ralph is a dog.
So Ralph barks.

Not Valid. "Only dogs bark" does not mean that all dogs bark.
It means that anything that barks has got to be a dog.

Some examples of *contradictories* (p. 29) of general claims :

All dogs bark.
Contradictory: Some dogs don't bark.

Some dogs bark.
Contradictory: No dogs bark.

Some dogs don't bark.
Contradictory: All dogs bark.

No women are truck drivers.
Contradictory: Some women are truck drivers.

Every Mexican likes vodka.
Contradictory: Some Mexicans don't like vodka.

Some Russians like chili.
Contradictory: No Russian likes chili.

Some whales eat fish.
Contradictory: Not even one whale eats fish.

Only dogs bark.
Contradictory: Some things that bark are not dogs.

If we want to say that just exactly dogs bark and nothing else, we should say that, or "Dogs and only dogs bark." The contradictory of that is "Either some dogs don't bark, or some things that bark aren't dogs."

Given the many ways to make general claims, we have only a rough guide for how to form their contradictories:

Claim	*Contradictory*
All —	Some are not — Not every —
Some —	No — All are not — Not even one —
Some are not —	All are —
No —	Some are —
Only S are P	Some P are not S Not every P is S

It is easy to get confused whether an argument using a general claim is valid. There are some methods that can help you discern whether some forms are valid or weak (see *Critical Thinking*.) Here are the most common valid forms, along with forms of weak arguments that are similar.

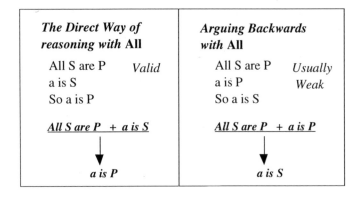

Valid: All dogs bark.   *Weak*: All dogs bark.
       Ralph is a dog.   Ralph barks.
       So Ralph barks.   So Ralph is a dog.

The argument on the right is arguing backwards. One way to be
something that barks is to be a dog, but there may be other ways
(seals and foxes).

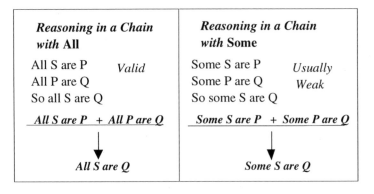

Valid: All dogs bark.
          Everything that barks is a mammal.
          So all dogs are mammals.

Weak: Some cats are faithful to their owners.
          Some things that are faithful to their owners are dogs.
          Therefore, some cats are dogs.

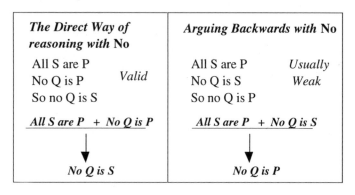

Valid: All dogs are mammals. *Weak*: All dogs bark.
No mammal lays eggs. No fox is a dog
So no dog lays eggs. So no fox barks.

Precise generalities are easy to evaluate in arguments (though percentages can cause other confusions, see pp. 56–57). For example:

72% of all workers at the GM plant say they will vote to strike. Harry works at the GM plant. So Harry will vote to strike.

Not strong. We can say exactly where this argument lands on the strong-weak scale: There's a 28% chance the premises could be true and conclusion false.

95% plus-or-minus 2% of all cat owners have cat-induced allergies. Dr. E's ex-wife has a cat. So very probably Dr. E's ex-wife has cat-induced allergies.

Strong. It's good if the premises are true.

Only 4% of all workers on the assembly line at the GM plant didn't get a raise last year. Wanda worked on the assembly line at the GM plant last year and this year. So Wanda almost certainly got a raise. *Strong.*

Vague generalities are difficult to reason with. They are usually too vague to make a claim. For example:

Most	Mostly	Many
A lot	Quite a lot	A bunch of
A few	A number of	

But two imprecise generalities are clear enough for us to use well in our reasoning:

Almost all   A very few

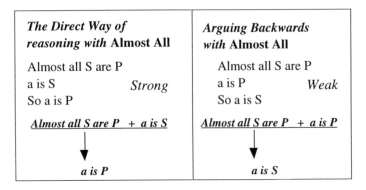

The Direct Way of reasoning with **Almost All**	*Arguing Backwards with* **Almost All**
Almost all S are P	Almost all S are P
a is S *Strong*	a is P *Weak*
So a is P	So a is S

Almost all parakeets are under 2' tall.
So the parakeets at Boulevard Mall are under 2' tall.
Strong.

Almost all university professors teach every year.
Mary Jane teaches every year.
So Mary Jane is a university professor.

Weak. Mary Jane could be a high school teacher. Compare to reasoning backwards with "all".

Reasoning in a chain with "almost all" is just as weak as reasoning in a chain with "some".

Almost all dogs like ice cream.
Almost all things that like ice cream don't bark.
So almost all dogs don't bark.
Weak.

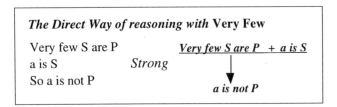

The Direct Way of reasoning with **Very Few**	
Very few S are P	
a is S *Strong*	
So a is not P	

Very few cats are loyal.
Puff is a cat.
So Puff is not loyal.
Strong.

All but a very few dogs don't bark.
Spot is Dick and Zoe's dog.
So Spot barks.
Strong. "Not" in the diagram means the contradictory.

The valid and weak forms using "no" become strong and weak forms using "a very few".

> All S are P.   *Strong*
> Only a very few Q are P.
> So only a very few Q are A.

All truck drivers have a commercial driver's license. Only a few beauticians have a commercial driver's license. So only a few beauticians are truck drivers.
Strong.

> All S are P.   *Weak*
> Only a very few Q are S.
> So only a very few Q are P.

All professors get a paycheck at the end of the month. Only a few people under 25 are professors. So only a few people under 25 get a paycheck at the end of the month.
Weak.

Some of the following examples are applications of the forms above, but many are not. Often you will just have to think your way through them. Remember, it's not whether the premises and conclusion happen to be true, but whether there are *possible* ways for the premises to be true and conclusion false.

Every newspaper that the Vice-President reads is published by an American publisher. All newspapers published by an American publisher are biased against Muslims. So the Vice-President reads only newspapers that are biased against Muslims.

Valid. Reasoning in a chain with "all".

Only managers can close out the cash register. George is a manager. So George can close out the cash register.
Invalid. "Only" does not mean "all". George could be a manager in charge of the stock room.

Everyone who wants to become a manager works hard. The people in Lois' group work hard. So the people in Lois' group want to become managers.
Invalid. Maybe the workers in Lois' group just want a raise and not the responsibility. (A weak form: All A are C; all B are C; therefore, all A are B.)

No taxpayer who cheats is honest. Some dishonest people are found out. So some taxpayers who cheat are found out.
Invalid. It could be that the only people who are found out are ones who steal.

Not every truck driver gets speeding tickets. Kim is a truck driver. So Kim doesn't get speeding tickets. *Weak.*

Some dogs bite mailmen. Some mailmen bite dogs. So some dogs and mailmen bite each other.
Invalid and weak. Maybe all the dogs who bite mailmen are terrified of the mailmen who would bite them.

All lions are fierce, but some lions are afraid of dogs. So some dogs aren't afraid of lions.
Invalid. Maybe the dogs don't recognize that the lions are afraid of them.

Some people who like pizza are vegetarians. Some vegetarians will not eat eggs. So some people who like pizza will not eat eggs.
Invalid and weak. Even though all the premises and the conclusion are true, the argument is bad. This is reasoning in a chain with "some".

No dogcatcher is kind. Anyone who's kind loves dogs. So no dogcatcher loves dogs.
Invalid. This is a bad argument, arguing backwards with "no".

No students are enthusiastic about mathematics. Harry is enthusiastic about mathematics. So Harry is not a student.
Valid, though bad. The direct way of reasoning with "no".

All nursing students take critical thinking in their freshman year. No heroin addict is a nursing student. So no heroin addict takes critical thinking his freshman year.
Weak. Reasoning backwards with "no".

Not every canary can sing. So some canaries can't sing.
Valid.

Some nursing students aren't good at math. John is a nursing student. So John isn't good at math.
Invalid, weak. John could be one of the nursing students who is good at math.

Every dog loves its master. Dick has a dog. So Dick is loved.
Valid.

Almost every dog loves its master. Dick has a dog. So Dick is loved.
Strong. A good argument.

Every cat sheds hair on its master's clothes. Dr. E does not have a cat. So Dr. E has no cat hair shed on his clothes.
Invalid. Dr. E could have picked up cat hair visiting a friend who has a cat.

No one who reads this book is going to beg in the street. Because only poor people beg. And people who read this book won't be poor because they understand how to reason well. *Good!*

10 Analogies

> A comparison becomes *reasoning by analogy*
> when it is part of an argument: On one side of
> the comparison we draw a conclusion, so on
> the other side we should conclude the same.

Should we let people who are HIV-positive remain in the military?
Sure, after all, Magic Johnson is playing in the NBA.

Analogy. This is an argument: Magic Johnson is allowed to play
in the NBA, so people who are HIV-positive should be allowed to
remain in the military.

We should legalize marijuana. After all, if we don't, what's the
rationale for making alcohol and tobacco legal?

Analogy. Alcohol is legal. Tobacco is legal. Therefore, marijuana
should be legal. They are sufficiently similar.

DDT has been shown to cause cancer in rats. Therefore, there is a
good chance DDT will cause cancer in humans.

Analogy. Rats are like humans. So if rats get cancer from DDT,
so will humans.

My love is like a red, red rose.

Not an analogy. What conclusion is being drawn?

An analogy is usually a weak argument. It will rely on
an implicit, unstated general principle. The value of the
analogy will be to force us to try to make that principle
explicit.

"Blaming soldiers for war is like blaming firemen for fires."

(Background: Country Joe MacDonald was a rock star who wrote songs protesting the war in Vietnam. In 1995 he was interviewed on National Public Radio about his motives for working to establish a memorial for Vietnam War soldiers in Berkeley, California, his home and a center of anti-war protests in the 60s and 70s. This claim was his response.)

Evaluation This is a comparison. But it's meant as an argument:

> We don't blame firemen for fires.
> Firemen and fires are like soldiers and wars.
> Therefore, we should not blame soldiers for war.

In what way are firemen and fires like soldiers and wars? They have to be similar enough in some respect for Country Joe's remark to be more than suggestive. We need to pick out important similarities that we can use as premises.

> *Firemen and fires are like soldiers and war.*
> wear uniforms
> answer to chain of command
> cannot disobey superior without serious consequences
> fight (fires/wars)
> work done when fire/war is over
> until recently only men
> lives at risk in work
> fire/war kills others
> firemen don't start fires—soldiers don't start wars
> usually like beer

That's stupid: Firemen and soldiers usually like beer. So?

When you ask "So?" you're on the way to deciding if the analogy is good. It's not just any similarity that's important. There must be some crucial, important way that firemen fighting fires is like soldiers fighting wars, some similarity that can account for why we don't blame firemen for fires that also applies to soldiers and war. Some of the similarities listed don't seem to matter. Others we can't use because they trade on an ambiguity, like saying firemen "fight" fires.

We don't have any good guide for how to proceed—that's a

weakness of the original argument. But if we are to take Country Joe MacDonald's remark seriously, we have to come up with some principle that applies to both sides.

The similarities that seem most important are that both firemen and soldiers are involved in dangerous work, trying to end a problem/disaster they didn't start. We don't want to blame someone for helping to end a disaster that could harm us all.

(‡) Firemen are involved in dangerous work.
Soldiers are involved in dangerous work.
The job of a fireman is to end a fire.
The job of a soldier is to end a war.
Firemen don't start fires.
Soldiers don't start wars.

But even with these added to the original argument, we don't get a good argument for the conclusion that we shouldn't blame soldiers for wars. We need a general principle:

You shouldn't blame someone for helping to end a disaster that could harm others, if he didn't start the disaster.

This general principle seems plausible, and it yields a valid argument.

But is the argument good? Are all the premises true? This is the point where the differences between firemen and soldiers might be important.

The first two premises of (‡) are clearly true, and so is the third. But is the job of soldiers to end a war? And do soldiers really not start wars? Look at this difference:

Without firemen there would still be fires.
Without soldiers there wouldn't be any wars.

Without soldiers there would still be violence. But without soldiers—any soldiers anywhere—there could be no organized violence of one country against another ("What if they gave a war and nobody came?").

So? The analogy shouldn't convince. The argument has a dubious premise.

We did not prove that soldiers should be blamed for wars. As always, *when you show an argument is bad you haven't proved the conclusion false.* You've only shown that you have no more reason than before for believing the conclusion.

Perhaps the premises at (‡) could be modified, using that soldiers are drafted for wars. But that's beyond Country Joe's argument. If he meant something more, then it's his responsibility to flesh it out. Or we could use his comparison as a starting place to decide whether there is a general principle, based on the similarities, for why we shouldn't blame soldiers for war.

Evaluating an Analogy

1. Is this an argument? What is the conclusion?
2. What is the comparison?
3. What are the premises (the sides of the comparison)?
4. What are the similarities?
5. Can we state the similarities as premises and find a general principle that covers the two sides?
6. Does the general principle really apply to both sides? What about the differences?
7. Is the argument strong or valid? Is it good?

The basic pattern of legal reasoning is reasoning by example. It is reasoning from case to case. It is a three-step process described by the doctrine of precedent in which a proposition descriptive of the first case is made into a rule of law and then applied to a next similar situation. The steps are these: similarity is seen between cases; next the rule of law inherent in the first case is announced; then the rule of law is made applicable to the second case.

Edward H. Levi, *An Introduction to Legal Reasoning*

11 Numbers

We use numbers to be exact, but it's easy
to be mislead when reasoning with them.

A vague or meaningless comparison gets no better by having
a few numbers in it—that's *apples and oranges.*

There were twice as many rapes as murders in our town.
Evaluation This seems to say something important, but what?

It's getting really violent here. There were 12% more murders this
year than last.
Evaluation This is also a mistaken comparison. If the town is
growing rapidly and the number of tourists is growing even faster,
it would be no surprise that the *number* of murders is going up,
though the *rate* (how many murders per 100,000 population)
might be going down. It's safer to live in a town of one million
that had 20 murders last year than in a small town of 25,000 that
had 6.

Two Times Zero Is Still Zero A comparison that
makes something look impressive, but the base of
the comparison is not stated.

A clothing store advertises a sale of sweaters at "25% off." You
take it to mean 25% off the price they used to charge which was
$20, so you'd pay $15. But the store could mean 25% off the
suggested retail price of $26, so it's now $19.50. You have to ask
"25% off *what*?"

Percentages can be misleading. For example:

Tom sees a stock for $60 and think it's a good deal. He buys it; a week later it's at $90, so he sells. He made $30—a 50% gain! His friend Wanda hears about it and buys the stock at $90; a week later it goes down to $60, so she panics and sells the stock. Wanda lost $30—that's a $33\frac{1}{3}$% loss. The same $30 is a different percentage depending on where you started.

$$50\% \uparrow \begin{bmatrix} \$90 \\ \$60 \end{bmatrix} \downarrow 33\frac{1}{3}\%$$

Often numbers are cited where it is clear *there is no way the number could be known.*

National Public Radio: "Breast feeding is up 16% from 1989."

Evaluation How could they know? Who was looking in all those homes? A survey? Whom did they ask? Women chosen randomly? But lots of them don't have infants. Women who visited doctors? But lots of women, lots of poor ones, don't visit their doctors.

What does "breast feeding" mean? Does a woman who breast feeds one day and then gives it up classify as someone who breast feeds? Or one who breast feeds two days? A month?

Maybe NPR is reporting on a reliable survey. But what they said is so vague and open to doubt as to how they could know it that we should ignore it as noise.

The *average* or *mean* of a collection of numbers is obtained by adding the numbers and then dividing by the number of items. The *median* is the midway mark: the same number of items above as below. The *mode* is the number most often obtained.

The *average* of 7, 9, 37, 22, 109, 9, 11 is calculated:
    Add $7 + 9 + 37 + 22 + 109 + 9 + 11 = 204$
    Divide   204 by 7 = 29.14, the average
The *median* is 11.
The *mode* is 9

An average is a useful figure to know only if there isn't too much variation in the figures. For example:

Dr. E's Final Exam

score	number of students
95	3 students
94	7 students
92	1 student
90	4 students
75	1 student
62	4 students
57	5 students
55	4 students
52	2 students

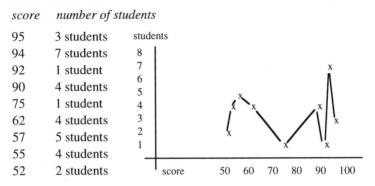

The grading scale was 90–100 = A, 80–89 = B, 70–79 = C, 60–69 = D, 59 and below = F. When Dr. E's department head asked him how the teaching went, he told her, "Great, just like you wanted, the average mark was 75%, a C." But she knows Dr. E too well to be satisfied. She asks him, "What was the median score?" Again Dr. E can reply, "75." As many got above 75 as below 75. But knowing how clever Dr. E is with numbers, she asks him what the mode score was. Dr. E flushes, "Well, 94." Now she knows something is fishy. When she asked that the average score be 75, she was thinking of a graph that looked like:

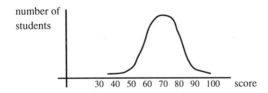

The distribution of the marks should be in a bell-shape: clustered around the median.

Unless you have good reason to believe that the average mark is pretty close to the median and that the distribution is more or less bell-shaped, the average doesn't tell you anything important.

12 Generalizing

We generalize every day, arguing from
a claim about some to a claim about more.

> **Generalizing** We are *generalizing* if we conclude a
> claim about a group, the **population**, from a claim about
> some part of it, the **sample**. To generalize is to make
> an argument.
>   Sometimes the general claim that is the conclusion
> is called the **generalization**; sometimes we call the
> whole argument a generalization.
>   The claims about the sample are called the
> **inductive evidence** for the generalization.

When we generalize from experience we cannot be certain of our conclusions. At best we can get a strong argument.

In a study of 5,000 people who owned pets in Anchorage, Alaska,
dog owners expressed higher satisfaction with their pets and with
their own lives. So dog owners are more satisfied with their pets
and their own lives than other pet owners.
Sample: The 5,000 people who were surveyed in Anchorage.
Population: Pet owners everywhere.

Of potential customers surveyed, 72% said that they liked "very
much" the new green color that Yoda plans to use for its cars. So
about 72% of all potential customers will like it.
Sample: The group of potential customers interviewed.
Population: All potential customers.
This is a *statistical generalization*.

Every time the minimum wage is raised, there's squawking that it will cause inflation and decrease employment. And every time it doesn't. So watch for the same bad arguments again this time.

Evaluation The unstated conclusion is that raising the minimum wage will not cause inflation or decrease employment. This is a generalization from the past to the future. *Sample:* All times in the past that the minimum wage has risen. *Population:* All times it has risen or will rise.

The doctor tells you to fast from 10 p.m. At 10 a.m. she gives you glucose to drink. Forty-five minutes later she takes some of your blood and has it analyzed. She concludes you don't have diabetes.
Sample: The blood the doctor took.
Population: All the blood you have in your body.

Wanda goes to the city council meeting with a petition signed by all the people who live on her block requesting that a street light be put in. Addressing the city council, she says, "Everyone on this block wants a street light here."
Not a generalization. There's no argument from some to more, since the sample equals the population.

Representative Sample A sample in which no one subgroup of the whole population is represented more than its proportion in the population.
A sample is *biased* if it is not representative.

Haphazard sampling Choosing the sample with no intentional bias. It may result in a representative sample, but we won't have any good reason to believe that the sample is representative.

To determine the attitudes of students about sex before marriage, Tom and three friends give a questionnaire to the first 20 students they meet coming out of the student union, the administration offices, and the largest classroom building at 9 a.m., 1 p.m., and 6 p.m. They are choosing a sample of students haphazardly. There is no reason to think the sample is representative.

> **Random Sampling**   A sample is chosen *randomly* if
> at every choice there is an equal chance for any one
> of the remaining members of the population to be picked.

If Tom assigns a number to each student, writes the numbers on
slips of paper, puts them in a fishbowl, and draws one number at a
time, that's probably going to be a random selection. But there's a
chance that slips with longer numbers will have more ink and fall
to the bottom of the bowl when you shake it. Or the slips aren't all
the same size. So typically to get a random selection we use tables
of random numbers prepared by mathematicians. Most spread-
sheet programs for home computers can generate tables of random
numbers. For Tom's survey he could get a list of all students; if
the first number on the table is 413 he'd pick the 413th student on
the list; if the second number is 711, he'd pick the 711th student on
the list; and so on, until he has a sample that's big enough.

Random sampling is likely to yield a sample that is
representative.

Suppose that of the 20,000 students at your college, 500 are gay
males. Then the chance that *one* student picked at random would
be a gay male is: $\dfrac{500}{20,000} = \dfrac{1}{40}$. If you were to pick 300 students
at random, the chance that half of them would be gay is very, very
small. It is very likely, however, that 7 or 8 ($1/40$ of 300) will be
gay males.

On the other hand, suppose roughly 50% of the students at
your college are female. Then each time you choose a student at
random there's a 50% chance it will be female. And if you randomly choose a sample of 300 students the chance is very high
that close to 50% will be female.

The *law of large numbers* says, roughly, that if the
probability of something occurring is X percent, then over
the long run the percentage of times that happens will be
about X percent.

The probability of a flip of a fair coin landing heads is 50%. So although you may get a run of 8 tails, then 5 heads, then 4 tails, then 36 heads to start, in the long run, repeating the flipping, if the coin is fair eventually the number of heads will tend toward 50%.

The gambler's fallacy A bad argument that a run of events of a certain kind makes a run of contrary events more likely in order to even up the probabilities.

Dick (at a roulette table): It's come up red 12 times in a row. It's bound to come up black several times in a row now.

Wrong. It could come up red 100 times in a row, and black could even out by coming up just one more time than red every 100 spins for the next 10,000 spins.

If you choose a large sample randomly, the chance is very high that it will be representative. That's because the chance of any one subgroup being over-represented is small—not nonexistent, but small. It doesn't matter if you know anything about the composition of the population in advance. After all, to know how many homosexuals there are, and how many married women, and how many men, and . . . you'd need to know almost everything about the population in advance. But that's what you need surveys for.

With a random sample we have good reason to believe the sample is representative. A sample chosen haphazardly may give a representative sample—but you have no good reason to believe it will be representative.

Weak Argument	*Strong Argument*
Sample is chosen *haphazardly*. Therefore, the sample is representative.	Sample is chosen *randomly*. Therefore, the sample is representative.
Lots of ways the sample could turn out to be biased.	Low probability the sample could turn out to be biased.

The classic example that haphazard sampling needn't work, even with an enormous sample, is the poll done in 1936 by *Literary*

Digest. The magazine mailed out 10,000,000 ballots asking who the person would vote for in the 1936 presidential election. They received 2,300,000 back. With that huge sample, the magazine confidently predicted that Alf Landon would win. Roosevelt received 60% of the vote, one of the biggest wins ever. What went wrong? The magazine selected its sample from lists of its own subscribers and telephone and automobile owners. In 1936 that was the wealthy class, which preferred Alf Landon.

Three premises are necessary, though not sufficient, for a generalization to be good.

Premises for a Good Generalization
The sample is representative.
The sample is big enough.
The sample is studied well.

Therefore: Generalization.

Sample Size The sample has to be big enough for a generalization to be good. Generalizing from a sample that is too small is called a *hasty generalization* or *anecdotal evidence*.

I've got a couple of Chinese students in my classes. They're both hard-working and get good grades. All Chinese must be like that.

But how big does a sample have to be? Roughly, the idea is to measure how much more likely it is that your generalization is going to be accurate as you increase the number in your sample. If you want to find out how many people in your class of 300 sociology students are spending 10 hours a week on the homework, you might ask 15 or 20. If you interview 30 you might get a better picture, but there's a limit. After you've asked 100, you probably won't get a much different result if you ask 150. And if you've asked 200, do you really think your generalization will be different if you ask 250? It hardly seems worth the effort.

Often you can rely on common sense when small numbers are involved. But when we generalize to a very large population, say 2,500, or 25,000, or 250,000,000, how big the sample should be cannot be explained without at least a mini-course on statistics. In evaluating statistical generalizations, you have to expect that the people doing the sampling have looked at enough examples, which is reasonable if it's a respected organization, a well-known polling company, physicians, or a drug company that's got to answer to the Food and Drug Administration. Surprisingly perhaps, 1,500 is typically adequate for the sample size when surveying all adults in the U.S.

However, how big the sample has to be depends on how much *variation* there is in the population. If there is very little variation, then a small sample chosen haphazardly will do. Lots of variation (or where you don't know how much variation there is) demands a very large sample, and random sampling is the best way to get a representative sample.

It's incredible how much information they can put on a CD. I just bought one that contains a whole encyclopedia.

Good generalization. Unstated conclusion: Every CD can contain as much information as this one that has an encyclopedia on it. There is little variation in the production of CDs for computers; a sample of one is sufficient.

The Sample is Studied Well The doctor taking your blood to see if you have diabetes won't get a reliable result if her syringe is contaminated or if she forgets to tell you to fast the night before. You won't find out the attitudes of students about sex before marriage if you ask a biased question. Picking a random sample of bolts won't help you determine if the bolts are O.K. if all you do is inspect them visually, not with a microscope or a stress test.

Questionnaires and surveys are particularly problematic. Questions need to be formulated without bias. Even then, you have to rely on the respondents answering truthfully.

Surveys on sexual habits are notorious for inaccurate reporting. Invariably the number of times that women in the U.S. report they engaged in sexual intercourse with a man in the last week, or month, or year is much lower than the reports that men give of sexual intercourse with a woman during that time. The figures are so different that it would be impossible for both groups to be answering accurately.

The Margin of Error and the Confidence Level It's never reasonable to believe exact statistical generalizations: 37% of the people in your town who were surveyed wear glasses, so 37% of all people in your town wear glasses. No matter how many people in your town are surveyed, short of virtually all of them, you can't be confident that exactly 37% of all of them wear glasses. Rather, "37%, more or less, wear glasses" would be the right conclusion.

That "more or less" can be made fairly precise according to a theory of statistics. The ***margin of error*** gives the range within which the actual number for the population is likely to fall. For example:

The opinion poll says that when voters were asked their preference, the incumbent was favored by 53% and the challenger by 47%, with a margin of error of 2%, and a confidence level of 95%. So the incumbent will win tomorrow.

From this survey they are concluding that the percentage of *all* voters who favor the incumbent is between 51% and 55%, while the challenger is favored by between 45% and 49%. The ***confidence level*** measures how likely it is that they're right. The confidence level here is 95%, which means that there is a 95% chance it's true that the actual percentage of voters who prefer the incumbent is between 51% and 55%. If the confidence level were 70%, then the survey wouldn't be very reliable: There would be a 3-out-of-10 chance the conclusion is false. Typically, if the confidence level is below 95%, the results won't be announced.

The bigger the sample, the higher the confidence level and the lower the margin of error. The problem is to decide how much it's worth in extra time and expense to increase the sample size in order to get a stronger argument.

Risk Risk doesn't change how strong an argument you have, only how strong an argument you want before you'll accept the conclusion.

With a shipment of 30 bolts, inspecting 5 and finding them O.K. would allow you to conclude that all the bolts are O.K. But if they're for the space shuttle, where a bad bolt could doom the spacecraft, you'd want to inspect each and every one of them.

Selective attention We can be mislead by how we pay attention.

It seems that buttered toast always lands the wrong side down, because you notice it when it does.

Examples

Every time I've seen a stranger come to Dick's gate, Spot has barked. So Spot will always bark at strangers at Dick's gate.
Bad generalization. The sample is haphazard. There's no reason to believe it's representative.

In a study of 5,000 people who owned pets in Anchorage, Alaska, dog owners expressed higher satisfaction with their pets and their lives. So dog owners are more satisfied with their pets and their own lives.
Bad generalization. The sample is clearly not representative. At best the evidence could lead to a conclusion about all pet owners in Anchorage, Alaska.

Maria has asked all but three of the thirty-six people in her class whether they've ever used heroin. Only two said "yes." So Maria concludes that almost no one in the class has used heroin.
Bad generalization. The sample is big enough and representative, but not studied well. People are not likely to admit to a stranger that they've used heroin; an anonymous questionnaire is needed.

My grandmother was diagnosed with cancer seven years ago. She refused any treatment that was offered to her over the years. She's perfectly healthy and doing great. The treatment for cancer is just a scam to get people's money.

Bad generalization. It's just anecdotal evidence.

Dick: A study I read said people with large hands are better at math.

Suzy: I guess that explains why I can't divide.

Bad application of a generalization. Perhaps the study was done carefully with a random sample. But you don't need a study to know that people with large hands do better at math: Babies have smaller hands, and they can't even add. *All people* is the wrong population to study.

Of chimpanzees fed one pound of chocolate per day in addition to their usual diet, 72% became obese within two months. Therefore, it is likely that most humans who eat 2% of their body weight in chocolate daily will become obese within two months.

Analogy. A generalization is needed to make this analogy good: 72% of *all* chimpanzees, more or less, will become obese if fed one pound of chocolate per day in addition to their usual diet. Whether this is a good generalization will depend on whether the researchers can claim that their sample is representative. The analogy then needs a claim about the similarity of chimpanzee physiology to human physiology.

13   Cause and Effect

We can establish some guidelines
for reasoning about cause and effect.

What exactly is a *cause*? Last night Dick said,

"Spot caused me to wake up."

Spot is the thing that somehow caused Dick to wake up. But
it's not just that Spot existed. It's what he was doing that
caused Dick to wake up: Spot's barking caused Dick to wake
up. So Spot's barking is the cause? What kind of thing is
that? The easiest way to describe the cause is to say,

"Spot barked."

The easiest way to describe the effect is to say,

"Dick woke up."

Causes and effects can be identified with claims.

This allows us to use all we know about claims in the
analysis of cause and effect, for instance whether they are
objective or subjective, and whether a sentence is too vague
to describe a cause or effect.

The relation of cause to effect requires that it be virtually
impossible for the cause to happen (to be true) and effect not
to happen (to be true). That's just the relation of premises to
conclusion in a valid or very strong argument. But here
we're not trying to convince anyone that the conclusion is
true: We know that Dick woke up. What we can carry over
from our study of arguments is how to look for all the
possibilities—all the ways the premises could be true and
conclusion false—to determine if there is cause and effect.

But the cause by itself is almost never enough to ensure that the effect follows.

A lot has to be true for it to be impossible for "Spot barked" to be true and "Dick woke up" to be false:

Dick was sleeping soundly up to the time that Spot barked.
Spot barked at 3 a.m.
Dick doesn't normally awake at 3 a.m.
Spot was close to where Dick was sleeping.
There was no other loud noise at the time.
  ⋮

We could go on forever. But as with arguments, we state what we think is important and leave out the obvious. If someone challenged us, we could add "There was no earthquake at the time"—but we just assume that.

The obvious unstated claims that are needed to establish cause and effect, comparable to unstated premises for an argument, are called the ***normal conditions.*** We can take claims as normal conditions only if they are obviously true and make the argument valid or very strong.

A ***causal claim*** is a claim that can be rewritten in the form "A causes (caused) B." "Spot caused Dick to wake up" is a ***particular cause and effect*** (causal claim). This happened once, then that happened once. Alternatively, we could generalize from this particular cause and effect to: "Very loud barking by someone's dog near him when he is sleeping *causes* him to wake, if he's not deaf." This is a ***general cause and effect*** claim. For it to be true, lots of particular cause and effect claims must be true. The normal conditions for this general claim won't be specific just to the one time Spot woke Dick, but will be general.

The police car's siren got me to pull over.
Particular causal claim. Cause: The police car had its siren going. Effect: I pulled over.

Because you were late, we missed the beginning of the movie.
Particular causal claim. Cause: You were late. Effect: We

missed the beginning of the movie.

Penicillin prevents serious infection.

Too vague. What is the cause? The existence of penicillin? It's that penicillin is administered to people in certain amounts at certain stages of their infections. Further, what's a "serious infection"?

Drinking coffee keeps people awake.

General causal claim. Cause: People drink coffee. Effect: People stay awake. Perhaps too vague.

Necessary Criteria for Cause and Effect

1. The cause precedes the effect.
2. It is impossible that the cause could be true and the effect false, given the normal conditions.
3. The cause makes a difference.
4. The cause is close in space and time to the effect.

The cause precedes the effect We wouldn't accept that Spot's barking caused Dick to wake up if Spot began barking only *after* Dick woke up. The cause has to precede the effect. That is, "Spot barked" became true before "Dick woke up" became true. For there to be cause and effect, the cause has to become true before the effect becomes true.

The cause makes a difference Dr. E has a desperate fear of elephants. So he buys a special wind chime and puts it outside his door to keep the elephants away. He lives in Cedar City, Utah, at 6,000 feet above sea level in a desert, and he confidently claims that the wind chime causes the elephants to stay away. After all, ever since he put up the wind chime he hasn't seen any elephants.

Why are we sure the wind chime being up did *not* cause elephants to stay away? Because even if there had been no wind chime, the elephants would have stayed away. Which elephants? All elephants. The wind chime works, but so would anything else. The wind chime doesn't make a difference. *For there to be cause and effect, it must be that if there were no cause, there would be no effect.* If Spot had not barked, Dick would not have woken up.

The cause is close in space and time to the effect   What is meant by "close" will depend on the circumstances, and you will have to use your judgment. The astronomer is right when she says that a star shining caused the image on the photograph, even though that star is very far away, and the light took millions of years to arrive. The problem isn't how distant in time and space the cause is from the effect. The problem is how much has come between the cause and effect—whether we can specify the normal conditions.

When we trace a cause too far back the problem is that the normal conditions begin to multiply. There are too many conditions for us to imagine what would be necessary to establish that it is impossible for the cause to have been true and effect false. When you get that far, you know you've gone too far.

Here are some *common errors* in reasoning about cause and effect.

Reversing cause and effect   If reversing cause and effect sounds just as plausible as the original claim, then we should investigate the evidence further before making a judgment.

— Sitting too close to the TV ruins your eyesight.
— How do you know?
— Well, two of my high school friends used to sit really close to the TV, and both of them wear really thick glasses now.
— Maybe they sat so close because they had bad eyesight.

Overlooking a common cause   We don't show a causal claim is false by raising the possibility of a common cause for both cause and effect. But we do put the claim in doubt. Then we have to use our judgment about which causal claim seems most likely.

— Zoe is irritable because she can't sleep properly.

— Maybe Zoe's both irritable and unable to sleep because she's been drinking so much espresso.

Looking too hard for a cause We look for causes because we want to understand, so we can control our future. But sometimes the best we can say is that it's ***coincidence***.

Before your jaw drops open in amazement when a friend tells you a piano fell on his teacher the day after your friend dreamt that he saw him in a recital, remember the law of large numbers: If it's possible, given long enough, it'll happen. After all, most of us dream—say one dream a night for fifty million adults in the U.S. That's three hundred and fifty million dreams per week. With the elasticity in interpreting dreams and what constitutes a "dream coming true," it would be amazing if a lot of dreams *didn't* "accurately predict the future."

But doesn't everything have a cause? Shouldn't we look for it? For much that happens in our lives we won't be able to figure out the cause—we just don't know enough. We must, normally, ascribe lots of happenings to chance, to coincidence, or else we have paranoia and end up paying a lot of money to phone psychics.

Post hoc ergo propter hoc ("after this, so because of this") A bad argument that there is cause and effect just because one claim became true after another.

I scored well on that last exam and I was wearing my red striped shirt. I'd better wear it every time I take an exam.

Every Tuesday and Thursday at 1:55 p.m. a tall red-headed lady walks by the door of Professor Zzzyzzx's classroom. Then he arrives right at 2 p.m. When Suzy says the lady walking by the door causes Professor Zzzyzzx to arrive on time at his class she's jumping to a conclusion: It happened after, so that's the cause.

The best prophylactic against making common mistakes in reasoning about causes is *experiment*. Often we can't do an experiment, but we can do an imaginary experiment. That's what we've always done in checking for validity: *Imagine the possibilities.*

How to look for a cause

Conjecture possible causes, and then by experiment eliminate them until there is only one. Check that one: Does it make a difference? If the purported cause is eliminated, is there still the effect?

Nancy caused the accident.

Evaluation: We're interested in who or what was involved in the cause when we go about assigning blame or fault. But it's not just that Nancy exists. Rather, the cause is: Nancy didn't pay attention; the effect is: The cars collided. Is this really cause and effect? Did the cause make a difference? If Nancy had been paying attention would the cars still have collided?

Lack of rain caused the crops to fail.

Evaluation Cause: There was no rain. Effect: The crops failed. This example was true a few years ago in the Midwest. Causes need not be something active; almost any claim that describes the world could qualify as a cause.

Oxygen in the laboratory caused the match to burn.

Evaluation Harry works in a laboratory where there's supposed to be no oxygen at all. The materials are highly flammable, and he has to wear breathing gear. He was joking around with a friend and struck a match, thinking it wouldn't ignite. There was an explosion. It seems there was a leak in his face mask.

The normal conditions don't include "Oxygen is in the laboratory." That, along with Harry striking the match, caused the match to burn. *There may be several claims we want to say jointly are the cause*: Oxygen was in the laboratory; Harry carried matches into the laboratory with him; Harry struck the match. The rest can be relegated to the normal conditions.

Running over nails causes your tires to go flat.

Evaluation This is a plausible general causal claim. But it's wrong. There's not good inductive evidence. Lots of times we run over nails and our tires don't go flat. But sometimes they do. What's correct is: "Running over nails *can cause* your tires to go flat." That is, if the conditions are right, running over a nail will cause your tire to go flat.

The difference between *causes* and *can cause* is the difference between the normal conditions. For "causes" we feel we don't need much that isn't obvious; for "can cause" we feel that we could list claims, but they aren't perhaps "normal" ones we daily expect, as discussed more in the next section, p. 75.

God caused the universe.

Evaluation This is not a causal claim. It's just a way of saying "God created the universe."

"When more and more people are thrown out of work, unemployment results." Calvin Coolidge

Evaluation This isn't cause and effect; it's a definition.

Birth causes death.

Evaluation This is a general causal claim covering every particular claim like: "That this creature was born caused it to die."
We have lots of inductive evidence: Socrates died. My dog Juney died. My teacher in high school died. President Kennedy died . . .

The problem seems to be that though this is true, it's uninteresting. It's tracing the cause too far back. Being born should be part of the normal conditions when we have the effect that someone died.

Zoe: Fear of getting fired causes me to get to work on time.

Evaluation What is fear? Cause: Zoe is afraid of getting fired.
Effect: Zoe gets to work on time.

Is it possible for Zoe to be afraid of getting fired and still not get to work on time? Certainly, but not, perhaps, under normal conditions: Zoe sets her alarm; the electricity doesn't go off; there isn't bad weather; Zoe doesn't oversleep; . . .

But doesn't the causal claim mean it's because she's afraid that Zoe makes sure that these claims will be true, or that she'll get to work even if one or more is false? She doesn't let herself oversleep due to her fear.

In that case how can we judge whether what Zoe said is true? It's easy to think of cases where the cause is true and effect false. So we have to add normal conditions. But that Zoe gets to work regardless of conditions that aren't normal is what makes her consider her fear to be the cause.

Subjective causes are often a matter of feeling, some sense that we control what we do. They are often too vague for us to classify as true or false.

Dick: Hold the steering wheel.
Zoe: What are you doing? Stop! Are you crazy?
Dick: I'm just taking my sweater off.
Zoe: I can't believe you did that. It's *so* dangerous.
Dick: Don't be silly. I've done it a thousand times before.
           Crash . . . Later
Dick: You had to turn the steering wheel!? That made us crash.

Evaluation The purported cause: Zoe turned the steering wheel. The effect: The car crashed. The necessary criteria are satisfied. But as they say in court, Zoe's turning the steering wheel is a *foreseeable consequence* of Dick making her take the wheel, which is the real cause. The normal conditions are not just what has to be true before the cause, but also what will normally *follow* the cause.

Dick: Wasn't that awful what happened to old Mr. Grzegorczyk?
Zoe: You mean those tree trimmers who dropped a huge branch
           on him and killed him?
Dick: You only got half the story. He'd had a heart attack in his
           car and pulled over to the side. He was lying on the pave-
           ment when the branch hit him and would have died anyway.

Evaluation What's the cause of death? Mr. Grzegorczyk would have died anyway. So the tree branch falling on him wouldn't have made a difference.

But the tree branch falling on him isn't a foreseeable consequence, part of the normal conditions of his stumbling out of his car with a heart attack. It's an *intervening cause.*

The Treaty of Versailles caused WWII.

Evaluation The cause: The Treaty of Versailles was agreed to and enforced. The effect: WWII occurred. To analyze a conjecture like this an historian will write a book. The normal conditions have to be spelled out. He has to show that it was a foreseeable consequence of the enforcement of the Treaty of Versailles that Germany would re-arm. But was it foreseeable that Chamberlain would back down over Czechoslovakia? More plausible is that the signing of the Treaty of Versailles is *a* cause, not *the* cause of WWII.

Poltergeists are making the pictures fall down from their hooks.

Evaluation   To accept this, we have to believe that poltergeists exist. That's dubious. Worse, it's probably not *testable*: How could you determine if there are poltergeists? Dubious claims that aren't testable are the worst candidates for causes.

Tom: The only time I've had a really bad backache is right after I went bicycling early in the morning when it was so cold last week. Bicycling never bothered me before. So it must be the cold weather that caused my back to hurt after cycling.

Evaluation.   Cause: It was cold when I went cycling. Effect: I got a backache. The criteria seem to be satisfied. But Tom may have overlooked another cause. He also had an upset stomach, so maybe it was the flu. Or maybe it was tension, since he'd had a fight with Suzy the night before. He'll have to try cycling in the cold again to find out. Even then it may be too much looking for *the* cause, when it may be *a* cause. Another possibility: Tom will never know for sure.

My neighbor said it's been the worst season ever for allergies this spring, but I told her I hadn't had any bad days. Then today I started sneezing. Darn it—if only she hadn't told me.

Evaluation   This may be cause and effect, but the evidence shouldn't convince. It's *post hoc ergo propter hoc* reasoning.

A recent study showed that everyone who uses heroin started with marijuana. So smoking marijuana causes heroin use.

Evaluation   And they all probably drank milk first, too. Without further evidence this is *post hoc ergo propter hoc.*

Cause in Populations

When we say, "Smoking causes lung cancer," what do we mean? If you smoke a cigarette you'll get cancer? If you smoke a lot of cigarettes this week, you'll get cancer? If you smoke 20 cigarettes a day for 40 years you'll get cancer? It can't be any of these, since we know smokers who did all that yet didn't get lung cancer, and the cause always has to follow the effect.

Cause in populations is usually explained as meaning that given the cause there's a higher probability that the effect will be true than if there were not the cause. In this example, people who smoke have a much higher probability of getting lung cancer. But really we are talking about cause and effect just as we did before. Smoking lots of cigarettes over a long period of time will cause (inevitably) lung cancer. The problem is that we can't state, we have no idea how to state, nor is it likely that we'll ever be able to state the normal conditions for smoking to cause cancer. Among other factors, there is diet, where one lives, exposure to pollution and other carcinogens, and one's genetic inheritance. But *if we knew exactly* we'd say: "Under the conditions _____, smoking ___ number of cigarettes every day for ___ years will result in lung cancer."

Since we can't specify the normal conditions, the best we can do is point to the evidence that convinces us that smoking is a cause of lung cancer and get an argument with a statistical conclusion: "People who continue to smoke two packs of cigarettes per day for ten years are ___ % more likely (with margin of error of ___ %) to get lung cancer."

Controlled experiment: cause-to-effect This is our best evidence. We choose 10,000 people at random and ask 5,000 of them never to smoke and 5,000 of them to smoke a pack of cigarettes every day. We have two samples, one composed of those who are administered the cause, and one of those who are not, the latter called the ***control group***. We come back 20 years later to check how many in each group got lung cancer. If a lot more of the smokers got lung cancer, and the groups were representative of the population as a whole, and we can see no other *common thread* amongst those who got lung cancer, we'd be justified in saying that smoking causes lung cancer. (Of course such an experiment would be unethical, so we use animals instead, and then argue by analogy.)

Uncontrolled experiment: cause-to-effect Here we take two randomly chosen, representative samples of the general population for which we have factored out other possible causes of lung cancer, such as working in coal mines. One of the groups is composed of people who say they never smoke. One group is composed of people who say they smoke. We follow the groups and 15–20 years later check whether those who smoked got lung cancer more often. Since we think we've accounted for other common threads, smoking is the remaining common thread that may account for why the second group got cancer more often.

This is a *cause-to-effect* experiment, since we start with the suspected cause and see if the effect follows. But it is uncontrolled: Some people may stop smoking, some may begin, people may have quite variable diets—there may be a lot we'll have to factor out in trying to assess whether it's smoking that causes the extra cases of lung cancer.

Uncontrolled experiment: effect-to-cause Here we look at as many people as possible who have lung cancer to see if there is some common thread that occurs in (almost all) their lives. We factor out those who worked in coal mines, we factor out those who lived in high pollution areas, those who drank a lot, . . . If it turns out that a much higher proportion of the remaining people smoked than in the general population, we have good evidence that smoking was the cause (the evaluation of this requires a knowledge of statistics). This is uncontrolled because how they got to the effect was unplanned, not within our control. And it is an *effect-to-cause* experiment because we start with the effect in the population and try to account for how it got there.

14 Fallacies

We've seen lots of bad arguments. Each fits *at least* one of the conditions for not repairing an argument or else directly violates the Principle of Rational Discussion. We picked out and labeled a few types of these as clearly unrepairable.

> ***Fallacy***   A bad argument of one of the types that have been agreed to be so bad as to be unrepairable.

Here are the fallacies discussed so far, along with a few others that are appeals to emotions. They are put into three categories.

Structural fallacies   Arguments that have one of the forms of a bad argument.

Affirming the consequent

Denying the antecedent

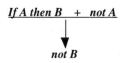

Arguing backwards with "all"

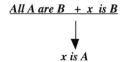

Arguing backwards with "almost all"

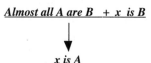

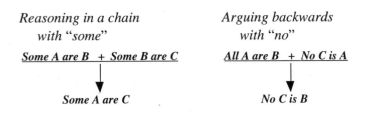

*Reasoning in a chain
with "some"*

Some A are B + Some B are C

Some A are C

*Arguing backwards
with "no"*

All A are B + No C is A

No C is B

Content fallacies   These are arguments that use (or require as unstated) a generic premise which, if false or very dubious, makes them bad. The appeals to emotions are listed first, with just the generic premise given, along with an example.

Appeal to pity
"You should believe or do ____ if you feel sorry for ____."
— You should vote for Ralph for school vice-president.
— Why?
— Because he doesn't have many friends, and it would make him feel good.

Appeal to fear (scare tactics)
"You should believe or do ____ if you are afraid of ____."

Dear Dr. E,
    I was very disappointed with my grade in your critical thinking course, but I'm sure that it was just a mistake in calculating my marks. Can I speak with you this Tuesday, right before I have lunch with my uncle, Dr. Jones, the Dean of Liberal Arts, where we plan to discuss sexual harassment on this campus?
                                      Sincerely, *Wanda Burnstile*

Appeal to spite
"You should believe or do ____ if you are mad about what ____ has done or believes."

Dick: Hi, Tom. What's wrong with your car?
Tom: The battery's dead. Can you help me push it?
       Harry will steer.
Dick: Sure.
Zoe: (whispering) What are you doing Dick? Don't you remember Tom wouldn't help you fix the fence last week?

Feel-good argument, apple polishing
"You should believe or do _____ if it makes you feel good."

I really deserve a passing grade in your course. I know that you're a fair grader, and you've always been terrific to everyone in the class. I admire how you handle the class, and I've enjoyed your teaching so much that it would be a pity if I didn't have something to show for it.

Wishful thinking is a feel-good argument you use on yourself.

Smoking can't cause cancer or I would have been dead a long time ago.

Calling in your debts
"You should believe or do _____ if you owe _____ a favor."

For an appeal to emotion to be a bad argument, the generic premise must be the only claim supporting the conclusion, where that isn't enough to justify the conclusion.

We should give to the American Friends Service Committee. They help people all over the world help themselves, and don't ask those they help whether they agree with them. They've been doing it well for nearly a century now. All those people who don't have running water or health care deserve our help. Poor little kids.

This is an appeal to pity. But it is a legitimate one.

Here are the other content fallacies discussed previously.

Appeal to authority
"(Almost) anything that _____ says about _____ is (probably) true."

Appeal to common belief
"If (almost) everyone else (in this group) believes it, then it's true."

Appeal to common practice
"If (almost) everyone else (in this group) does it,
then it's O.K. to do."

Confusing objective and subjective
"This claim is subjective." / "This claim is objective."

Drawing the line
"If you can't make this difference precise, there is no
difference."

False dilemma
Reasoning by excluding possibilities, but the "or" claim is
false or very dubious.

Gambler's fallacy
A run of events of a certain kind makes a run of contrary
events more likely in order to even up the probabilities.

Mistaking the person (group) for the claim
"(Almost) anything that _____ says about _____ is false."

Mistaking the person (group) for the argument
"(Almost) any argument that _____ gives about _____ is bad."

Phony refutation
"_____ has done or said _____, which shows that he or she
does not believe the conclusion of his or her own argument"
and "If someone does not believe the conclusion of his or
her own argument, the argument is bad."

Post hoc ergo propter hoc
"This happened after that, so it's cause and effect."

Slippery slope
(Reasoning in a chain with conditionals where one of them is
false or enough of them are dubious so that the conclusion
doesn't follow.)

Violations of the rules of rational discussion   Some of
these aren't fallacies, because they aren't arguments. But
they're collected here for ready reference of bad ways to
convince.

Begging the question
The point of an argument is to convince that a claim is true.
So if the premises of an argument are no more plausible than
the conclusion, it's a bad argument.

Relevance
Sometimes people say a premise or premises aren't relevant
to the conclusion. But that's not a category of fallacy, just an
observation that the argument is so weak you can't imagine
any way to repair it.

Ridicule
Making someone or something the butt of a joke in order to
convince.

Strawman
It's easier to knock down someone's argument if you
misrepresent it, putting words in the other person's mouth.

Shifting the burden of proof
It's easier to ask for a disproof of your claim than to prove it
yourself.

Slanters
Concealing claims that are dubious by misleading use of
language.

These labels for bad arguments are like names that go on
pigeon holes: This bad argument can go in here, that argument there, this one fits into perhaps two or three of the
pigeon holes, this argument, no, it doesn't fit into any, so
we'll have to evaluate it from scratch. If you forget the

labels, you can still remember the style of analysis, how to look for what's going wrong. That's what's important. The labels are just shorthand for doing the hard work of explaining what's bad in an argument.

You've learned a lot of labels and can manage to make yourself unbearable to your friends by pointing out the bad arguments they make. That's not the point.

We want to learn, to exchange ideas, not stifle disagreements. We want to convince and educate, and to that end we must learn to judge bad arguments.

Some arguments are so bad there's no point in trying to repair them. Start over.

Some arguments are bad because the other person intends to mislead you. In that case the Principle of Rational Discussion is violated. There's no point continuing the discussion. These labels and analyses are then prophylactics against being taken in.

But often enough the person making the bad argument isn't aware that he or she has changed the subject or brought in emotions where they don't belong. Be gentle. Point out the problem. Educate. Maturity isn't pointing a finger at someone and laughing. Ha, ha. Ask the other person to fill in the argument, to add more claims. Then you can, perhaps, learn something, and the other person can, too.

15 Evaluating Arguments

> We can summarize the methods for evaluating
> the various ways of reasoning studied here.

Arguments

1. First read the entire passage and decide if there's an
   argument. If so, identify the conclusion and number every
   sentence or clause that might possibly be a claim.

2. For each numbered part, decide if it is a claim:
   a. Is it too vague or ambiguous?
   b. If it's vague, could we clear that up by looking at the
      rest of the argument? Are the words implicitly defined?
   c. If it's too vague, scratch it out as noise.
   d. If it uses slanters, reword it neutrally.

3. Identify the claims that lead directly to the conclusion.

4. Identify any subarguments that are meant to support
   the claims that lead directly to the conclusion.

5. See if the obvious objections have been considered.
   a. List ones that occur to you as you read the passage.
   b. See if they have been answered.

6. Note which claims in the argument are unsupported,
   and evaluate whether they are plausible.

7. Evaluate each subargument on the scale from valid to strong through weak.
   a. Note if the argument is one of the bad types or valid types we've discussed.
   b. If it is not valid or strong, can it be repaired?
   c. If it can be repaired, do so and evaluate any added premises.
8. Evaluate the entire argument as valid, strong, or weak. Repeat (a)–(c) of (7) for the entire argument.
9. Decide whether the argument is good.

That's a lot to do. But not all the steps are needed each time. If you spot that you have an argument that is one of the bad types we've discussed, you can dismiss it. If key words are too vague to consider the conclusion or crucial parts as claims, you can dismiss the reasoning. But often you'll have to go through all these steps. Or you could just go with your gut reaction—throwing out all the work you've done in learning to reason well. Remember: It is irrational to accept that the premises of an argument are plausible and the argument is good, yet still reject the conclusion. If you think there's something wrong with an argument, find it.

Here are the methods of evaluation for the particular kinds of arguments and reasoning discussed in this book.

Analogies

1. What is the comparison?

2. What are the premises (the sides of the comparison)?

3. What are the similarities?

4. Can we state the similarities as premises and find a general principle that covers the two sides?

5. Does the general principle really apply to both sides? What about the differences?

6. Evaluate the passage using the steps for arguments.

Generalizing

1. Identify the sample and the population.
2. Are the three premises for a generalization plausible?
   a. The sample is representative.
   b. The sample is big enough.
   c. The sample is studied well.
3. Evaluate the passage using the steps for arguments.

Cause and Effect Reasoning

1. Identify the purported cause and effect as claims. Are they too vague? Could we clear that up by looking at the rest of the passage? Are the words implicitly defined?
2. Decide if the inference from cause to effect is valid or very strong. (Use the methods for evaluating arguments.)
3. Decide if the cause precedes the effect.
4. Decide whether the cause makes a difference: If there were no cause, would the effect still be true?
5. Make sure that none of the obvious mistakes are made:
   a. It's not cause and effect reversed.
   b. It's not overlooking a common cause.
   c. It's not *post hoc ergo propter hoc*.
   d. It's not mistaking coincidence for cause and effect.
6. Decide whether you can conclude there's cause and effect.

Cause in Populations

1. Identify the kind of experiment that is used to support the conclusion: controlled or uncontrolled; cause to effect, or effect to cause.
2. Decide whether you should accept the results of the experiment.
   a. Was it conducted well? (Use the methods for evaluating generalizations.)
   b. Does it really support the conclusion? (Use the steps for evaluating arguments and cause and effect.)
3. Decide whether the argument is good.

16 Writing Good Arguments

If you can't spell, if you can't write complete sentences, if you leave words out, then you can't convince anyone. All the reader's effort will be spent trying to decipher what you intended to say.

If you don't have an argument, literary style won't salvage your essay.

If the issue is vague, use definitions or rewrite the issue completely to make a precise claim to deliberate.

Don't make a clear issue vague by appealing to some common but meaningless phrase, such as "This is a free country."

Beware of questions used as claims. The reader might not answer them the way you do.

Your premises must be highly plausible, and there must be glue, something that connects the premises to the conclusion. Your argument must be impervious to the questions: So? Why?

Don't claim more than you actually prove.

There is a trade-off: You can make your argument strong, but perhaps only at the expense of a rather dubious premise. Or you can make all your premises clearly true, but leave out the dubious premises that are needed to make the argument strong. Given the choice, opt for making the argument strong. If it's weak, no one should accept the conclusion. And if it's weak because of unstated premises, it is better to have those premises stated explicitly so that they can be the object of debate.

Your reader should be able to follow how your argument is put together. Indicator words are essential.

Your argument won't get any better by weaseling with "I believe that" or "I feel that." Your reader probably won't care about your feelings, and they won't establish the truth of your conclusion.

Your argument should be able to withstand the obvious counterarguments. It's wise to consider them in your essay.

For some issues, the best argument may be one which concludes that we should suspend judgment.

Slanters turn off those you might want to convince—you're preaching to the converted. Fallacies just convince the careful reader that you're dumb or devious.

You should be able to distinguish a good argument from a bad one. Use the critical abilities you've developed to read your own work. Learn to stand outside your work and judge it, as you would judge an argument made by someone else.

17 Making Decisions

The skills you've learned here can help you make better decisions.

Making a decision is making a choice. You have options. Make a list for and against the claim—all the pros and cons you can think of. Make the best argument for each side. Then your decision should be easy: Choose the option for which there is the best argument. Making decisions is no more than being very careful in constructing arguments for your choices.

But there may be more than two choices. Your first step should be to list all the options and give an argument that these really are the only options, and not a false dilemma.

Suppose you do all that, and you still feel there's something wrong. You see that the best argument is for the option you feel isn't right. You have a gut reaction that it's the wrong decision. Then you're missing something. Don't be irrational. You know when confronted with an argument that appears good yet whose conclusion seems false, you must show that the argument is weak or a premise is implausible. Go back to your pro and con lists.

Now that your reasoning has been sharpened, you can understand more, you can avoid being duped. And, we hope, you will reason well with those you love and work with and need to convince. And you can make better decisions. But whether you will do so depends not just on method, not just on the tools of reasoning, but on your goals, your ends. And that depends on virtue.

Index

About the author
Richard L. Epstein received his B.A. *summa cum laude* from
the University of Pennsylvania in 1969, and his Ph.D. in
Mathematics from the University of California, Berkeley in
1973. He held a Postdoctoral Fellowship in Mathematics and
Philosophy at the University of Wellington, New Zealand
from 1975–1977. In 1978 he took a position in the Mathematics Department of Iowa State University and received
tenure there in 1981. In 1982 he returned to the University
of California, Berkeley as a Visiting Professor in
Mathematics while studying more general problems in the
foundations of reasoning under the tutelage of Benson Mates.
He has been a U.S. National Academy of Sciences Scholar to
Poland, and a Fulbright Fellow to Brazil. He now writes
books on logic and reasoning.

Other books by Richard L. Epstein
published by Wadsworth:

Critical Thinking
Predicate Logic (The Semantic Foundations of Logic)
Propositional Logics (The Semantic Foundations of Logic)
Computability
The Pocket Guide to Reasoning in the Sciences
Five Ways of Saying "Therefore" (2000)
Reasoning in the Sciences (2001)